World's Worst Serial Killers

DAVID ELIO MALOCCO

Copyright © 2014 David Elio Malocco

All rights reserved.

ISBN: 1499702701
ISBN-13: 978-1499702705

DEDICATION

To Colette

CONTENTS

	Acknowledgments	I
1	Introduction	Page 8
2	Definition of a Serial Killer	Page 10
3	What Make a Serial Killer?	Page 17
4	The Ten Most Depraved	Page 26
5	Top 50 Serial Killers	Page 145
6	Bibliography	Page 195

ACKNOWLEDGMENTS

The Arts Council of Ireland

Much of the material for this book has been taken from five previous books written by the author including:
Serial Sex Killers: Real American Psychos (2014)
Sexual Psychopaths: British Serial Killers (2014)
Murder for Profit: They Killed for Money (2014)
Who's Who Serial Killers (2014)

All of these books are available on Amazon, Barnes & Noble, Eason, Lulu and Kindle.

CHAPTER ONE
AN INTRODUCTION

How do you know if you are living next door to a psychopath? The short answer is that you don't. Psychopaths have the ability to compartmentalize their lives. One moment they might be hosting a child's birthday party; the next strangling one of the mother's to death in the bathroom. They do not have the emotions we have. In fact, they do not have any emotions. This is why they are so difficult to catch. They don't follow a normal pattern. Take Dennis Rader as an example.

On the face of it Dennis was a normal, happily married man with two children who lived in a compact detached family home in the suburbs. He had a steady job. He had no criminal convictions. He appeared to adore his wife. Neighbors often commented on how pleasant and courteous he was. He was a loyal and faithful husband. He didn't abuse alcohol or drugs and he didn't fool around. He was a respected member of society. But Dennis was also a psychopath, rapist, sexual predator and serial killer. He enjoyed torturing his victims. Afterwards, he would tidy up and go home to his loving family and no one was any the wiser. Not even his wife of thirty four years.

Dennis is one of over fifty serial killers profiled in this book. Some like John Wayne Gacy, Ted Bundy, Gary Ridgway, H. H. Holmes, Richard Ramirez, Harold Shipman, Ed Gein and Albert Fish are names you probably know well. But there are many others you may not know. This book brings their lives right up to date.

The book is split into two parts. The first part profiles in detail the top ten most evil and sadistic serial killers of all time including Albert Fish, H. H. Holmes, Ted Bundy, Ed Gein, Richard Ramirez, Fred and Rose West, Jeffrey

Dahmer, Lawrence Bittaker and Richard Trenton Chase. These ten are chosen because they are regarded as the world's most depraved, evil and sadistic serial killers ever.

The second section details the fifty worst serial killers of all time based on the number of their actual kills. The rankings are based on real identifiable evidence. The book tries not to sensationalize their crimes or endeavor to explain their actions. Nor does it judge them.

That is for you to do.

CHAPTER TWO
DEFINITION OF SERIAL KILLER

All multiple murders are categorized into three types; serial, mass or spree murders. Essentially, there are two main differences between the categories. The first is the amount of time that elapses between killings. The second is the geographic distance over which the murders occur.

Mass murder is defined by the Federal Bureau of Investigation (FBI) as: "A number of murders, (four or more), occurring during the same incident, with no distinctive time period between the murders. These events typically involve a single location where the killer murders a number of victims in an on-going incident." A similar definition is provided by Fox and Levin (2005) – who define mass murder as an offence in which there are at least four victims killed in the same general area at one time.

Spree killing relates to the killing of multiple victims over a period of time in two or more locations and often occurs in conjunction with other criminal behavior.

Somewhat surprisingly, there is, as yet, no universal definition of what constitutes a serial killer. As Mouzos and West (2008) maintain that there is a lack of consensus among academics and practitioners in the definition of serial murder. They cite various experts when they argue that disagreement centers on the number of victims, the presence or absence of a sexual element, and the common characteristics of victims.

Other experts like Harbort and Mokros (2001) argue that despite the term *serienmörder* which is German for serial murderer, being used since the early 1930s, with reference to Peter Kurten, its exact meaning is not completely clear, especially for the purposes of research. They point to the controversy surrounding the defining criteria of a serial killer, citing Egger (1984) who suggests the term includes all those who have committed a second and/or subsequent murder. On the other end of the scale Dietz (1986) argues that the term should apply only to those who kill others in ten or more separate incidents.

In an effort to bridge the gap between the many views of issues related to serial murder, the FBI hosted a multi-disciplinary Symposium in San Antonio, Texas. The goal of the Symposium, which took place between 29 August and 2 September 2005, was to bring together a group of respected experts on serial murder from a variety of fields and specialties in the hope of being able to identify common denominators with regard to serial killing. The agenda comprised of a variety of topics related to serial murder including, amongst others, common myths, definitions, typologies, pathology and causality, forensics, prosecution issues, and major case management issues. Much of the general public's knowledge regarding serial murder is a product of outlandish Hollywood movies.

Screenplays and the story lines within them are created for the sole purpose of heightening the interest of audiences. They are not written with a view to accurately portray serial murder. Such productions tend to sensationalize the atrocities inflicted on victims by "deranged" offenders, thus striving to ensure that the audience becomes captivated by the killers and their heinous crimes. This simply fuels the fires of confusion to the true dynamics of serial killers. It also perpetuates the common myths and misconceptions surrounding serial killing.

Contrary to popular myth serial killers are not all dysfunctional loners. Many are married, have families and mortgages, are gainfully employed and appear to be normal members of the community. It is because they have the ability to assimilate themselves into the very fabric of society that they are often overlooked by law enforcers and the police.

John Wayne Gacy was a pillar of society, happily married with children who ran three KFC franchises, was chairman of the Jaycees and undertook a lot of charity work as *Pogo the Clown*. John also murdered at least thirty three young men and buried twenty six in the crawl space underneath his house.

Robert Yates was married with five children, lived in a middle class neighborhood, and was a decorated U.S. Army National Guard helicopter pilot. He also murdered seventeen prostitutes in the Spokane, Washington area, during the 1990s. Bob even buried one of his victims in his garden underneath his bedroom window. He was eventually arrested and pleaded guilty to thirteen of the murders.

Gary Ridgway, confessed to killing forty eight women over a twenty-year time period in the Seattle, Washington area. He had been married three times and was still married at the time of his arrest. He worked for thirty two years as a painter. He was a regular Church goer, read the Bible at home and at work, and talked about religion with his fellow workers. Gary was also addicted to prostitutes.

Again, contrary to popular belief, not all serial killers are motivated by sex. Although most of the serial killers profiled in this book are all sexual deviants, killers motivated by sex-lust, there are many other motivations for serial murders. These include anger, thrill, financial gain, and attention seeking. George Metesky, the *Mad Bomber of New York*, killed because he was angry with the Con Ed Company for letting him go after an accident and then with society at large for ignoring his claim for justice. John George Haigh, the *Acid Bath Murderer*, murdered six people so he could sell their possessions and keep all their money. Ian Brady and Myra Hindley, the *Moors Murderers*, killed for kicks.

Another popular myth is that once they start serial killers cannot stop killing. However, there are many instances where serial killers stop murdering altogether before being caught. In these instances, there are events or circumstances in offenders' lives that inhibit them from pursuing more victims. These can include increased participation in family activities, sexual substitution, and other diversions. For example, Dennis Rader, the *BTK* killer, (BTK stands for Blind, Torture, Kill), murdered ten victims from 1974 to 1991. He then retired. He did not kill any other victims prior to being captured in 2005. During interviews conducted by law enforcement, Rader admitted to engaging in auto-erotic activities as a substitute for his killings.

Hollywood would have us believe that all serial killers are either insane or evil geniuses. As a group, serial killers suffer from a variety of personality disorders, including psychopathy, anti-social personality, and others. However, the vast majority of serial killers are not considered insane under the law. Nor are they "evil geniuses" outsmarting law enforcers at every turn. Like any other group, serial killers range in intelligence from borderline to above average.

Another myth is that serial killers want to get caught. They may express that sentiment when they get caught, but they don't mean it. Each time they kill they gain experience and confidence until they eventually succeed with the minimum mistakes or problems. Most are highly organized. They plan, select, target, approach, control, and dispose of their victims. The logistics involved in killing and then disposing of a body are highly complex. After they have killed several times they become empowered, feeling they will never be identified. It is not the case that serial killers want to get caught; they feel that they can't get caught.

As regards a definition, the different discussion groups at the FBI Symposium agreed on a number of similar factors to be included in a definition. These include:
one or more offenders
two or more murdered victims
incidents should be occurring in separate events, at different times
the time period between murders separates serial murder from mass murder

In combining the various ideas put forth at the Symposium, the following definition was crafted:

Serial Murder: The unlawful killing of two or more victims by the same offender(s), in separate events.

Mouzos and West (2007) reviewed the literature on serial killers with a view to drawing up a set of common characteristics while Kraemer, Lord and Heilbrun (2004) suggest that serial murder has been described as deliberate, premeditated and sexually predatory in nature with a lack of interpersonal conflict and provocation. This description appears to argue that all serial killings are organized. But the evidence suggests otherwise. All the killings carried out by Peter Kurten were disorganized.

Nor are all killings motivated by sex. There does not appear to be any sexual element in the murders committed by Harold Shipman although his murders were quite clearly premeditated. Whilst there is a clear sexual element in the murders committed by Peter Kurten, the degree of premeditation appears to vary from murder to murder, with the killing of Christine Klein appearing to be purely opportunistic.

Meanwhile, Folino (2000) is not surprised by this confusion. He believes that the characteristics of serial killers, their behavior, actions and motivations are diverse, intricate and include cross cultural variations. This contention appears to be borne out by the statistics. The United States contains only 5% of the world's population but based on available data, it produces 76% of the world's total of serial killers. Europe produces the second highest number at 17% with Britain producing 28% of the European total, closely followed by Germany on 27%. In the United States, California has the highest serial killer rate while Maine has the lowest.

Sex killing is synonymous with the paraphilic term erotophonophilia which basically means the sexual arousal or gratification of a person which is contingent on the death of a human being. Frequently this type of killing manifests itself either during sexual intercourse and/or by mutilating the sexual organs or areas of the victim's body. The mutilation of the victim, which usually takes place post mortem, may include evisceration and/or displacement of the genitalia.

Often serial sex killers remove clothing from the body. Sometimes they pose or prop the body in different positions, often sexually explicit ones. It is not uncommon for objects to be inserted into bodily orifices. Nor is it uncommon to expect anthropophagy, the consumption of human blood and/or flesh or necrophilia, the performing of sex acts on a human corpse. For the most part sex killers involve male perpetrators.

Usually sex killers make a connection between murder and sexual gratification. When this type of killer chooses a victim there is usually something about that victim that the killer finds either sexually attractive or sexually repulsive. This attractive trait might be common among all of the killer's victims and is referred to as the killer's IVT or Ideal Victim Type.

Once the killer has located an IVT he might first engage in stalking that victim before acting out his fantasy. Fantasy constitutes a common factor in sex killings. However, such fantasies can never be completely fulfilled. That's why sex killers tend to retain a fantasy that continues to evolve over time and becomes increasingly violent as they struggle to fulfil it. Sometimes the killing experience generates new fantasies of violence, creating a repetitive cycle. The purpose of fantasy is to gain total control of the victim; whereas the purpose of sexual assault is merely a vehicle for control.

Sex killers use sexual torture as a tool to degrade, humiliate, and subjugate the victim. But the term can also be used in a related but slightly different sense and that is to refer to an individual who gains sexual arousal from the act of committing murder, or has persistent sexual fantasies of committing murder. This book provides examples of some of the world's most depraved serial sex killers.

CHAPTER THREE
WHAT MAKES A SERIAL KILLER?
THE PSYCHOLOGY OF SEXUAL PREDATORS

"No one ever suddenly became depraved." - Juvenal

CHILDHOOD

Why do some people become serial killers while others do not? Well, it seems that several factors can contribute to the creation of a serial sex killer. The first and most revealing place psychiatrists look at is the childhood and upbringing of the serial killer. Some endured horrific upbringings. Peter Kurten was born into abject poverty in 1883 in Koln-Mulheim a suburb of Koln in Germany.

The eldest of thirteen children, his father was a sadistic alcoholic who frequently abused his wife, physically and sexually, in the one roomed flat they all shared, during the duration of Peter's childhood. His father would come home drunk and force his wife to strip and have sex with him in front of the children. It was almost a daily occurrence. Who could doubt that his sadistic impulses were awakened by the violent scenes in his own home?

Albert De Salvo was born in 1931. He was one of six children of Frank De Salvo, an alcoholic laborer, and Charlotte, his wife. The family lived in Chelsea, a poor, working class area of Boston. His father often brought prostitutes home. He was a bully of a man who was physically abusive to his wife and children. When he was just seven De Salvo watched as his father brutally attacked his mother, dislodging her teeth. He then proceeded to bend back her fingers, one by one, until they snapped. The family were so poor that Frank De Salvo sold Albert and two of his sisters as slaves to a Maine farmer for the sum of nine dollars a day. It took them several months to escape. He then forced all his children to steal, whether by shoplifting, burglary or robbery. In a desperate effort to raise money for his family Albert resorted to selling his body to local homosexuals.

Rose West was born in 1953 in Barnstaple, Devon, England to William Letts and Daisy Fuller. She was one of three daughters. Her father who was in the army was a strict disciplinarian who was known to bully his wife. Her parents argued frequently and when they did William would beat his wife. But, it wasn't just his wife he beat. He regularly found reasons to beat his children, violently throwing one down the stairs and banging another's head against a brick wall. If his wife intervened she would become the target of his uncontrollable rage. During one such intervention he threw a pot of boiling water over her.

Berry-Dee (2007) argues that a lot of people suffer as children and most grow out of it. They develop into decent, law-abiding and valuable members of society. In his opinion, serial killers make the same mistakes over the course of their lives and they cannot make the transition into adulthood. Serial killers want to feel important and they want to feel special. Most of all they crave the sense of power, dominance and control. However, it is precisely because they cannot achieve this power, dominance and control in a respectable and honest way that they resort to killing, torturing, sodomizing and dismembering innocent people. By carrying out those acts they then feel good about themselves.

It is generally accepted that the structure and quality of family interaction is an important part of the development in any child. This is particularly so in the way the child itself perceives family members. According to the FBI who have carried out studies on this: "For children growing up, the quality of their attachments, to parents and to other members of the family, is most important as to how these children, as adults, relate to and value other members of society. Essentially, these early life attachments (sometimes called bonding) translate into a map of how a child will perceive situations outside the family."

There can be little doubt that a traumatic childhood characterized by physical and/or sexual abuse may be a strong contributory factor in the development of the serial killer or rapist. However, evidence provided by the lack of such behavior in the offender's brothers and sisters, or in the fact that such abuse is not evident in the early childhood of other serial killers, like, for example, Dennis Nilsen, strongly suggests that a traumatic childhood in itself, is not a sufficient explanation for the crimes committed by serial killers.

Some parents believe that if they are harsh disciplinarians it will have the effect of toughening up their child. But it doesn't. Instead, it leads to an absence of love between parent and child, an absence that can have disastrous results. As the FBI has said, if the child doesn't bond with its primary caretakers, with whom will it bond? There is absolutely no foundation for trusting anyone else later in life. The result leads to isolation, where intense violent fantasies become the primary source of gratification.

Ressler, Douglas and Burgess wrote in their book Sexual Homicide: Patterns and Motives: "Instead of developing positive traits of trust, security, and autonomy, child development becomes dependent on fantasy life and its dominant themes, rather than on social interaction." According to Ressler et al., when the child grows up, all they know are their fantasies of domination and control. They have not developed compassion for others. Instead, humans become flattened-out symbols for them to enact their violent fantasies.

However, contrasting studies have shown that the majority of sexually sadistic murderers had no evidence of childhood abuse So, what other factors are involved?

JUVENILE REHABILITATION

Many serial killers have claimed that the abuse they received in "Care" Homes, "Reform" Schools and "Rehabilitation" Centers played a major factor in turning them against society. Albert Fish spent most of his childhood in an orphanage. Rather than reform him Fish began to enjoy the physical pain that the beatings brought. Speaking about his sadistic treatment in the orphanages he once said: "I was there till I was nearly nine, and that's where I got started wrong. We were unmercifully whipped. I saw boys doing many things they should not have done."

Although 1920's killer Carl Panzram was an incorrigible juvenile delinquent, the brutal torture he received in reform school aggregated his violent rage. This is how he described his treatment and the reaction to it: "From the treatment I received while there and the lessons I learned from it, I had fully decided when I left there just how I would live my life. I made up my mind that I would rob, burn, destroy and kill everywhere I went and everybody I could as long as I lived. That's the way I was reformed ..."

Peter Kurten's juvenile criminal career secured him a total of twenty seven prison sentences. The crimes were petty, larceny of food and clothes and he was sent to various Reform schools. Rather than reform him the experience left him bitter, twisted and extremely angry at the penal conditions that adolescents were forced to endure. He later said about his time in reform school: "It was then that I became acquainted with disciplinary punishment in prison, and of the severest kinds. It was terrible what I suffered under it. I would describe it all as barbarous and I suppose most men would do so today. Hunger in adolescence is real torture...I do not condemn those sentences in themselves, but I do condemn the way they are carried out on young people...Fettering was a common form of punishment. Once I was fettered for three weeks...All that had a very bad effect on me, so I can tell of these things in full justification. Nothing is worse than the spiritual suffering of one who is tortured through the infliction of pain."

INSANITY

Are serial killers insane? By legal standards few of them are. In his 1976 book Murder and Madness psychiatrist Donald Lunde states that the incidence of psychosis among murderers is no greater than the incidence of psychosis in the total population. Lunde is a psychiatrist who teaches at Stanford University. He explains that the legal definition of insanity is based on the 19th century McNaghten Rules: Does the offender understand the difference between right and wrong?

If he flees or makes any attempt to hide the crime, then the offender is not insane, because his actions show that he understood that what he was doing was wrong. In an interview in People magazine by Nancy Faber in August 1977 he was asked if most mass murders are insane: "Most are mentally ill, but insanity is a legal term, not a medical one. Herbert Mullin, who shot or knifed thirteen people, including a Catholic priest, was diagnosed as a paranoid schizophrenic by all the psychiatrists who examined him, both for the defense and the prosecution. Yet he was found sane at his trial and sent to prison."

So, should the legal definition of insanity be changed? Lunde believes that it probably should, but none of the formulas suggested so far have proved satisfactory: "The criticism of the existing standard of insanity, the McNaghten rule of 1843, is that it leaves out the emotional factor. You are found to be sane if you have the intelligence to understand the questions, 'Did you know that was a gun in your hand and not a banana you were squeezing?' or, 'Do you know that killing is wrong?' The rule was written long before psychiatry was born."

In the case of Albert Fish, who was quite obviously deranged, the jury found him "insane, but he deserved to die anyway." Is there something inherently bad in serial killers? Are some people born with a killer gene?

NATURAL BORN KILLERS

Some commentators believe that the reasons why certain people commit serial murder are biological, suggesting serial killers are born not made. They claim that the violent behavior exhibited by serial killers is as a result of abnormal brain activity. Cesare Lombroso was one such commentator. Lombroso was born in Verona on the 6 November 1835 and his fame rests, above all, on his theory of the atavistic or born criminal, the individual whose physical structure possesses the degenerative traits that differentiate him from the normal, socially well-adjusted man.

His general theory suggested that criminals are distinguished from non-criminals by multiple physical anomalies. He claimed that criminals represented a reversion to a primitive or subhuman type of man characterized by physical features reminiscent of apes which he called modern day savages.

Lombroso was convinced that the "born criminal" or *reo nato* a term coined by one of his students, Enrico Ferri, could be anatomically identified by such features as a sloping forehead, ears of unusual size, asymmetry of the face, prognathism (protrusion of the lower jaw), excessive length of arms, asymmetry of the cranium, and other "physical stigmata". He claimed that criminals had a lack of moral sense, including an absence of remorse, more vanity, impulsiveness, vindictiveness, and cruelty. They also possessed other manifestations, such as a special criminal argot and the excessive use of tattooing.

However, towards the end of his career he gave some recognition to psychological and sociological factors in the etiology of crime, but he remained convinced of, and mostly identified with, criminal anthropometry. Today, most of his theories have been widely discredited.

It is highly unlikely that any child is born with a killer gene that turns them into a depraved serial killer. Something usually happens, or more than likely, a combination of events occur, at a very young age, which will send them over the edge. In an article published in the Journal of Contemporary Criminal Justice (August 1999) Holmes, Tewksbury and Holmes proposed a new theory of serial murder combining elements of Cooley's Looking Glass Self and Goffman's Virtual and Actual Social Identity calling it "Fractured Identity Syndrome" (FIS).

In doing so, their purpose was to get the profession to begin to think about and develop theories concerning what causes the serial murderer to abandon normal modes of behavior and brutally take the lives of his or her victims. Fractured Identity Syndrome suggests that during childhood or adolescence, an important event, or series of events results in a fracturing of the personality of the serial killer. The term "fracture" is defined as a small breakage of the personality which is often not visible to the outside world and is only felt by the child.

"Social Process Theory" has also been suggested as an explanation for serial murder. According to this theory criminal behavior is a function of a socialization process. This theory suggests that offenders turn to crime as a result of peer group pressure, family problems, poor school performance, legal entanglements and other situations that gradually steer them towards criminal behavior. This theory posits that anyone can become a criminal.

The main support of this theory stems from the effect of the family on youths who engage in delinquent or violent behavior. Researchers believe there is a link between childhood experiences of violence and behavioral problems. In these experiences, children can be victims or eyewitnesses. According to the theory, children who witness family violence are more likely to display diminished social competence and behavioral problems than those who do not. What about head injuries sustained to individuals in the course of their lives?

BRAIN DEFECTS

It is surprising how many serial killers have suffered severe head injuries in their lives. Bobby Joe Long who suffered a severe head injury following a motorcycle accident once commented: "After I'm dead, they're going to open up my head and find that just like we've been saying a part of my brain is black and dry and dead." John George Haigh, the *Acid Bath Murderer*, suffered head injuries in a car accident. Fred West also had a motor cycle accident and a further accident when he fell ten feet from an outside fire escape and landed on his head. He spent seven days in a coma as a result of the first accident and twenty four hours in a coma as a result of the second. Friends and families claimed that he underwent a significant personality changes as a result of these accidents. As a child, Ken

Bianchi fell off of a jungle gym, and landed on the back of his head. He soon began to have epileptic seizures. Other serial killers who suffered head injuries include Leonard Lake, David Berkowitz, John Wayne Gacy, and Carl Panzram.

According to many researchers, brain defects and injuries have been an important link to violent behavior. When the hypothalamus, the temporal lobe, and, or the limbic brain show damage, it may account for uncontrollable rage or aggression. But brain damage does not provide a guarantee that the sufferer will evolve into a serial killer. Many people who suffer brain injuries remain non-violent.

CONCLUSION

While experts have identified traits and abnormalities common to serial killers, there are many who possess these traits and do not go on to become serial killers. So, what is it then that leads some to act on their deviant fantasies while others do not? In the end, all we can conclude is that serial killers possess black holes in their psyche. They appear to be so normal, so generic, so invisible, yet they terrify us simply because they mirror us.

Perhaps we should leave the last word to Henry Lee Lucas who once grimly proclaimed: "All across the country, there's people just like me, who set out to destroy human life."

Let's meet some

CHAPTER FOUR
THE TEN MOST DEPRAVED

1. ALBERT HAMILTON FISH (1870-1936)

"I am a man of passion. You don't know what that means unless you are my kind. At the orphanage they put me just before Garfield was assassinated, there were some older boys that caught a horse in a sloping field. They got the horse up against a fence down at the bottom of the field and tied him up. An old horse. They put kerosene on his tail and lit it and cut the rope. Away went that old horse, bursting through fences to get away from the fire. But the fire went with him. That horse, that's me. That's the man of passion. The fire chases you and catches you and then it's in your blood. And after that, it's the fire that has control and not the man. Blame the fire of passion for what Albert H. Fish has done."

- Albert H. Fish in The Daily News 12 March 1935

Albert Hamilton Fish known as *The Grey Man* was a sexual pervert, sadist, cannibal, child killer and probably American's most infamous serial killer ever. He claimed to have tortured, mutilated and killed at least one child in every American State before his eventual capture. He ate the bodies of many of his victims. He claimed he had killed one hundred children. But was he insane?

He was born on the 19 May, 1870, in Washington, D.C. into a middle class family. His father was Captain Randall Fish, a Potomac River boat captain who later made and sold fertilizer. His mother, Ellen, was of Scots-Irish ancestry. His father was forty three years older than his mother and was seventy five when Albert was born. He had three siblings who lived, Walter, Annie and Edwin. His father dropped dead on the 15 October 1875. There was no doubt that Fish came from a flawed pedigree. Psychosis was rampant in the family tree. One uncle, on his father's side, suffered from a religious psychosis and died in a state hospital. His half-brother also died in a state hospital. A younger brother was feeble-minded and died of hydrocephalus, commonly known as water on the brain. His mother was, in his own words, considered to be "very queer" and suffered from auditory and visual hallucinations. An aunt, on his father's side, was completely crazy while his brother was afflicted with chronic alcoholism. Finally, one of his sisters suffered from a mental disorder.

When he was five his mother placed him in St. John's Orphanage in Washington where he remained until he was nine when his mother secured a State job and could afford to take him out. He said of the orphanage that the experience, the violence and hunger, completely changed him. He witnessed boys being whipped. He saw teachers forcing the youths in their care to strip and then masturbating them in front of the other children. This was his first sexual experience.

By seventeen he was sent out in the world on his own. He travelled to Europe and became a male prostitute in Brussels, servicing both men and women. Fish was basically a homosexual; women were only a means to vent certain perverse feelings. When he returned to America he began working at a variety of odd jobs. His main trade was painting, but his real vocation was to indulge in as many perverse pleasures as he could, his preference being children. Later in 1890 he moved to New York and worked as a painter. He brought his mother up from Washington and they lived at 76 West 101st Street. His mother introduced him to his wife and they had six children, Albert, Anna, Gertrude, Eugene, John, and Henry Fish. She later left him in 1917 and went off with a lodger called John Straube. He then became responsible for the six children.

Fish began molesting children, mostly young boys, as early as 1890 and engaged in every type of sexual perversion known to man including urolagnia, drinking urine and coprophagia, eating feces. Although he was based in New York his painting business took him elsewhere and he travelled around extensively.

In 1911, during a stay in St. Louis, Fish sexually molested an intellectually disabled nineteen year old man called Kedden. He had tied him up and tried to castrate him with a pair of scissors but abandoned the task half way through and fled the city leaving the victim $10 for his suffering. By this time Fish was well known in the brothels of New York city where his favorite treat was sadomasochism. He loved to inflict pain on others and have pain inflicted on himself.

After his wife left him Fish began to seriously indulge in self harm. He would embed needles into his body between his scrotum and anus and leave them there; repeatedly beat himself with a nail-studded paddle; and insert wool doused with lighter fluid into his anus and then light it. But the most perverse of all was his practice, which his psychiatrist Dr. Wertham describe as "unique", of inserting the stem of a rose into his penis. He would then stand before the mirror and look at himself before eating the rose.

Some of these he inflicted on his victims. He claimed to have abducted, tortured and killed at least one hundred boys in different states all over America. Some of these he ate. His *modus operandi* was simple and logical. Fish would bribe them with money or sweets. He usually chose African-American children because he believed that the police did not pay much attention when they were hurt or went missing. He adhered to a strict code of rules. For example, he never went back to the same neighborhood twice.

He claimed to have lived in at least twenty three states and that he had killed at least one child in each state. When he was under suspicion he would simply move on to another state and another child. But it was the high profile abductions of Grace Budd, Francis McDonnell and Billy Gaffney that would eventually be his downfall.

In July 1924, eight year old Francis McDonnell was playing on the front porch of his home in the Charlton Woods area of Staten Island. His mother was sitting nearby nursing her infant daughter. While looking out onto the road she noticed a gaunt old man with grey hair and a grey moustache. Several hours later a third party noticed an old man with a similar description watching Francis playing ball with four other boys. The old man called Francis over to him and the other boys continued to play ball. Moments later the boys noticed that both Francis and the old man had vanished.

Francis was found shortly afterwards, hidden under some branches in a nearby wood. He had been stripped, badly beaten and strangled with his suspenders. In fact, he was so badly beaten that police had doubts that the old grey haired man could have been solely responsible. However, despite the extensive manhunt the Grey Man simply vanished.

In February 1927 four year old Billy Gaffney disappeared. The Gaffneys occupied a small dimly lit apartment on the second floor of 99 Fifteenth Street, a run-down tenement building situated between Third and Fourth Avenue in Brooklyn. On Friday the 11 February Billy Gaffney had been playing in the hallway outside his apartment with his three-year-old neighbor who was also called Billy, Billy Beaton. A third neighbor, Johnny McNiff, who was just twelve was minding his sleeping baby sister. He left her for a moment to go to the two children who were playing. He then heard his sister cry so he returned to her. Moments later he noticed that Billy Gaffney and Billy Beaton were both gone. He went to Billy Beaton's father and told him the boys were missing.

His father immediately went looking for the two boys believing they may have wandered out to the busy street below. He eventually discovered his son alone on the top floor of a building and asked him where Billy Gaffney was. But all the boy would say was: "The bogey man took him." The police were called in and began an extensive search. Eventually, someone had the foresight to question the three year old again. When asked again he repeated that the bogey man had taken Billy Gaffney. He was then asked to describe the "bogey man". He said he was a slender old man who had grey hair and a grey moustache. Yet again, the police failed to make any connection with this grey man and the grey man who was involved in an abduction a few years previously

Albert Budd Sr. was a porter for the Equitable Life Assurance Company who lived with his family in a small apartment at the rear of a poor tenement at 406 West 15th Street in Manhattan in New York. Albert was married to Delia, a tall, large lady who had borne him five children, Edward, Albert Junior, George, Grace and baby Beatrice. He worked hard but they barely survived above the poverty line.

His eldest son, Edward, a strong, strapping and enterprising eighteen year old decided he didn't want to spend another summer in the hot, stinking poverty of New York City and on the 25 May 1928 placed an ad in the *New*

York World newspaper looking for summer work in the country. The following Monday a small, elderly man who introduced himself as Frank Howard called to his home and offered him and his friend, Willie, a job for the summer on his farm in Farmingdale in Long Island. He said he would call back in a week to collect them.

When he did call back he was introduced to their beautiful ten year old daughter Grace. Frank explained that he had to go that evening to his sisters for a birthday party for one of his children but would be back later to collect Edward and Willie. As he was walking out the door he asked the Budds if Grace would like to go to the party up at Columbus and 137th Street. Although they hesitated they felt that since he was Edward's new employer and they had met him twice that it was fine by them.

That was the last time they ever saw Grace. Police investigators told them there was no farmer called Frank Howard in Long Island and no such farm existed. Columbus didn't reach as far as 137th street; no such address existed. The old, kind and friendly man was a fraud. The abduction of Grace Budd now made the front page of newspapers across America. Eventually, the case went cold. Neither Grace, nor the man who called himself Frank Howard, could be found. And soon, Gracie Budd just became another unsolved statistic on the files of New York's Missing Persons Bureau, at least for now.

In November 1934, the Grace Budd abduction case, while six year old, was officially still open although nobody other than veteran detective William King believed it could be solved. King was friendly with the hugely popular newspaper columnist Walter Winchel and asked him to place a piece about Grace in his column "On Broadway," published in the *New York Daily Mirror*. As a result of this article the Budds received a particularly vile letter.

It read: "My dear Mrs. Budd, In 1894 a friend of mine shipped as a deck hand on the Steamer Tacoma, Capt. John Davis. They sailed from San Francisco for Hong Kong China. On arriving there he and two others went ashore and got drunk. When they returned the boat was gone. At that time there was famine in China. Meat of any kind was from $1 to $3 a pound. So great was the suffering among the very poor that all children under 12 were sold for food in order to keep others from starving. A boy or girl under 14 was not safe in the street. You could go in any shop and ask for steak, chops, or stew meat.

Part of the naked body of a boy or girl would be brought out and just what you wanted cut from it. A boy or girls behind which is the sweetest part of the body and sold as veal cutlet brought the highest price. John staid there so long he acquired a taste for human flesh. On his return to N.Y. he stole two boys one seven, one eleven. Took them to his home stripped them naked tied them in a closet. Then burned everything they had on. Several times every day and night he spanked them, tortured them, to make their meat good and tender. First he killed the 11 year old boy, because he had the fattest ass and of course the most meat on it. Every part of his body was Cooked and eaten except the head, bones and guts. He was Roasted in the oven (all of his ass), boiled, broiled, fried and stewed. The little boy was next, went the same way.

At that time, I was living at 409 E 100 st., near — right side. He told me so often how good Human flesh was I made up my mind to taste it. On Sunday June the 3rd 1928 I called on you at 406 W 15 St. Brought you pot cheese — strawberries. We had lunch. Grace sat in my lap and kissed me. I made up my mind to eat her. On the pretense of taking her to a party. You said Yes she could go. I took her to an empty house in Westchester I had already picked out. When we got there, I told her to remain outside. She picked wildflowers. I went upstairs and stripped all my clothes off. I knew if I did not I would get her blood on them.

When all was ready I went to the window and called her. Then I hid in a closet until she was in the room. When she saw me all naked she began to cry and tried to run down the stairs. I grabbed her and she said she would tell her mamma.

First I stripped her naked. How she did kick, bite and scratch. I choked her to death, then cut her in small pieces so I could take my meat to my rooms. Cook and eat it. How sweet and tender her little ass was roasted in the oven. It took me nine days to eat her entire body. I did not fuck her though I could of had I wished. She died a virgin."

Nobody wanted to believe that this letter was true. It had to be the ravings of some perverted, sadistic lunatic. But, Detective King was aware that the details contained in the letter of his meeting with the Budds and Grace were accurate. They had a lead and that lead brought them a clue. The clue was not in the body of the letter; it was on the envelope. On the envelope there was a small hexagonal emblem with the letters N.Y.P.C.B.A. which stood for the New York Private Chauffeur's Benevolent Association. King eventually traced Fish to his old rooming house at 200 East 52nd Street and on the 13 December 1934 arrested him for the abduction and murder of Grace Budd.

The confession of Albert Fish would be heard by many people, detectives, attorneys and psychiatrists. They had never heard anything like it before and probably never would again. Described as "an odyssey of perversion and depravity" it was grotesque, unbelievable, bizarre and unprecedented. That was, until detail after detail was corroborated. It was all the more amazing considering how decrepit and harmless Albert Fish appeared. He was a stooped, frail-looking old man about five-feet, five-inches tall. Fish admitted to killing Grace in Westchester and later brought them to where he had buried her remains.

He admitted to strangling her and then undressing her. He put her body on a table and with the help of the cleaver and butcher's knife he began the considerable task of dismembering her body. He began by cutting it in half. Bodies were more manageable that way. He took sections of the body with him having wrapped them in old newspapers. He left the remaining parts in the house until he returned several days later.

Some of her body he threw over a stone wall in the back of the house. He disposed of his instruments in the same manner. When he had finished his confession, King asked him what had caused him to do such a horrible thing? Fish gave the following simple reply: "You know, I never could account for it."

Albert Fish faced indictments in Manhattan and Westchester County. Westchester County indicted him first on a charge of first degree murder, while Manhattan was preparing an indictment for kidnapping. Meanwhile police enjoyed a really major break. The motorman on the Brooklyn trolley line saw a picture of Fish in the newspaper. He made a statement identifying Fish as the nervous old man that he saw on the 11 February, 1927. He was trying to keep a little boy who was sitting beside him quiet. Joseph Meehan, the retired motorman, watched the two carefully. He noticed that the little boy was not properly attired. He didn't have a jacket or coat, and was crying for his mother continuously. He had to be dragged by the old man on and off the trolley. As it turned out the little boy in question was the kidnapped Billy Gaffney.

Eventually, when his fate was already sealed Fish made a confession admitting the abduction and murder of Billy Gaffney: "I brought him to the Riker Ave. dumps. There is a house that stands alone, not far from where I took him... I took the boy there. Stripped him naked and tied his hands and feet and gagged him with a piece of dirty rag I picked out of the dump.

Then I burned his clothes. Threw his shoes in the dump. Then I walked back and took the trolley to 59 St. at 2 A.M. and walked from there home.

Next day about 2 P.M., I took tools, a good heavy cat-of-nine tails. Home made. Short handle. Cut one of my belts in half, slit these halves in six strips about eight inches long. I whipped his bare behind till the blood ran from his legs. I cut off his ears, nose, slit his mouth from ear to ear. Gouged out his eyes. He was dead then. I stuck the knife in his belly and held my mouth to his body and drank his blood.

I picked up four old potato sacks and gathered a pile of stones. Then I cut him up. I had a grip with me. I put his nose, ears and a few slices of his belly in the grip. Then I cut him through the middle of his body. Just below the belly button. Then through his legs about two inches below his behind. I put this in my grip with a lot of paper. I cut off the head, feet, arms, hands and the legs below the knee. This I put in sacks weighed with stones, tied the ends and threw them into the pools of slimy water you will see all along the road going to North Beach."

The confession was so awful it seemed as if it couldn't be true, but it was. This frail, meek old man had done this and worse: "I came home with my meat. I had the front of his body I liked best. His monkey and pee wees and a nice little fat behind to roast in the oven and eat. I made a stew out of his ears, nose, pieces of his face and belly. I put onions, carrots, turnips, celery, salt and pepper. It was good.

Then I split the cheeks of his behind open, cut off his monkey and pee wees and washed them first. I put strips of bacon on each cheek of his behind and put them in the oven. Then I picked four onions and when the meat had roasted about 1/4 hour, I poured about a pint of water over it for gravy and put in the onions. At frequent intervals I basted his behind with a wooden spoon. So the meat would be nice and juicy.

In about two hours, it was nice and brown, cooked through. I never ate any roast turkey that tasted half as good as his sweet fat little behind did. I ate every bit of the meat in about four days. His little monkey was a sweet as a nut, but his pee-wees I could not chew. Threw them in the toilet."

Once his photograph appeared in all the dailies other witnesses came forward. A man from Staten Island identified Fish as the man who had tried to lure his then eight-year-old daughter into the woods not far from where Francis O'Donnell was murdered three days later in 1924. The girl, in her late teens, saw him in his cell and recognized him. Finally, the man known as the *Grey Man* had been captured.

Later he was also tied to the 1932 murder of a fifteen year old girl named Mary O'Connor in Far Rockaway. The girl's mauled body was found in some woods close to a house that Fish had been painting.

With the proliferation of indictments in different counties there was very little chance that Albert Fish was ever going to be acquitted. His only opportunity to beat the death penalty was to be declared insane something the authorities did not want to happen. His attorney employed two of America's finest psychiatrists to support the plea of insanity, Smith Ely Jelliffe and Frederick Wertham. But could they save Fish from the electric chair?

Wertham had no problem giving his expert opinion that the accused, his patient, Albert Fish was legally insane. He described what he had done after cutting Grace's body into little pieces. He wrapped the body parts in a piece of old newspaper and carried them back to his rooms. Simply by holding this package on his lap, as he rode the train home, gave him such a sexual high that caused him to spontaneously ejaculate. As soon as he got back to his rooms he proceeded to cut the child's flesh into smaller pieces and used them to make a stew which he infused with carrots, onions and bacon.

He stretched the stew out to last nine days to enhance the pleasure as long as he could. During all of this time he had retained a state of sexual heaven which necessitated him to masturbate several times a day. He would savor the food at night while he lay awake in the darkness and masturbate himself to sleep. Then as soon as he awoke the following day the sexual arousal would begin again. Wertham knew Fish was insane but could he convince the court and jury?

On the 11 March 1935 the trial of Albert Fish opened in White Plains, New Jersey with Justice Frederick P. Close presiding. In sports parlance, it was a sell-out. Following the successful conviction of Bruno Richard Hauptmann for the kidnapping and murder of the Charles Lindberg baby the Fish trial now took center stage as the most newsworthy event of the year. Fish was charged with the pre-meditated murder of Grace Budd. Chief Assistant District Attorney Elbert F. Gallagher was in charge of the prosecution and James Dempsey was the defense attorney.

Gallagher said he was sane; that he knew what he was doing and that he knew it was wrong. He was bad not mad. This was the central point of the trial.

Under cross examination Gallagher put it to Wertham that the defendant knew the difference between right and wrong and therefore legally was sane. He asked the question: Didn't his cunning, in trying to conceal his crimes, not indicate that he was intelligent enough to know the difference? It was a clever question. But Wertham had an even more clever reply. He said that Fish was certainly intelligent enough to understand the consequences of his crimes and to take precautions against discovery and subsequent arrest. But to really know the difference between right and wrong requires a "certain emotional sympathy. You have to feel what is right and wrong."

Dr. Wertham went on to explain his patient's mental stability in the following terms: "This defendant is suffering from mental disease. He is so mixed up about the question of punishment, of sin, of atonement, of religion, of torture that he is in a particularly bad state to know the difference between right and wrong. He is even worse off than that, because he actually has a perverted, a distorted, if you will, an insane, knowledge of right and wrong."

Two other defense psychiatrists, Smith Ely Jelliffe and Henry A. Riley corroborated what Wertham had said about Fish. Their medical opinion was clear: Albert Fish was insane.

The trial lasted ten days and the jury took less than an hour to reach its verdict. "We find the defendant guilty as charged," the foreman said. The judge had no option but to sentence the accused to death by way of electrocution. Less than a year after his trial, Hamilton Albert Fish ate his last meals. He had T-bone steak for lunch with the bone removed as a precaution against self-harm. In the evening he had roast chicken. Once again the bones were removed so as to prevent self-harm. However, by this stage he had lost his appetite and only had a few mouthfuls of food. Shortly after 11:00 p.m. on the 16 January, 1936 Fish was strapped into the chair and executed by Robert Elliott the official executioner, another grey man.

MAD OR BAD

Of all the psychiatrists that interviewed Fish, Wertham was the one that spent the most time with him. He visited him three times in Eastview spending a total of twelve hours attempting to analyze him. He described his first meeting with the accused in his jail cell in his book The Show of Violence. Wertham was shocked at how "meek, gentle, benevolent and polite" Fish was. "If you wanted someone to entrust your children to, he would be the one you would choose." Fish's attitude towards his situation was one of complete detachment. At one point in the interview he said: "I have no particular desire to live. I have no particular desire to be killed. It is a matter of indifference to me. I do not think I am altogether right."

When Dr. Wertham asked him if he thought he was insane Fish replied: "Not exactly, I compare myself a great deal to Harry Thaw in his ways and actions and desires. I don't understand myself. It is up to you to find out what is wrong with me." In June 1906 Thaw shot and killed the architect Stanford White on the roof of Madison Square Garden. White had actually been the architect for the building. He shot him having discovered that White was sleeping with his wife, Evelyn Nesbit, a former showgirl. He was declared criminally insane and served just nine years in an institution. He had employed as an expert witness none other than Smith Ely Jelliffe.

Wertham discovered that what drove Fish most of all was the infliction of pain not just on others but also on himself. As Wertham says: "Sado-masochism directed against children, particularly boys, took the lead in his sexually regressive development."

Fish told him that he always had a desire to inflict pain on others and to have others inflict pain on him. He always seemed to enjoy everything that hurt. He practiced every imaginable kind of experience with excreta, actively and passively. For example, he would take clumps of cotton, saturate them with alcohol, insert them into his rectum, and then set fire to them. He would also do this with his child victims. He claimed to have had at least one hundred boys in different states all over America. It is uncertain whether he meant he had sexually abused them or murdered them or both.

Fish suffered from a second compulsion, a compulsion to write obscene letters and did so frequently. According to Dr. Wertham: "the letters were not the typical obscene letters based on fantasies and daydreams to supply a vicarious thrill. They were offers to practice his inclinations with the people he wrote his graphic suggestions to."

Initially, Wertham found it difficult to believe that Fish was telling him the truth. An experienced criminal psychiatrist, he was well aware of the propensity of serial killers to lie and exaggerate. This was especially so when Fish began to tell him about his habit of sticking needles into his body, a habit he had "enjoyed" for many years.

He told the doubting psychiatrist that he would stick needles in the area between his rectum and the scrotum: "He told of doing it to other people too, especially children. At first, he said, he had only stuck these needles in and pulled them out again. Then he had stuck others in so far that he was unable to get them out, and they stayed there." Curious as to whether Fish was being truthful or playing with him Wertham had him x-rayed. To his amazement the x-ray showed up at least twenty nine needles in his pelvic region.

So far, Fish had demonstrated that he had known the difference between right and wrong which meant that legally speaking he was sane but then Fish began relating how from the age of fifty five he had begun to experience hallucinations and delusions. Wertham relates these experiences in his book: "He had visions of Christ and His angels... he began to be engrossed in religious speculations about purging himself of iniquities and sins, atonement by physical suffering and self-torture, human sacrifices... He would go on endlessly with quotations from the Bible all mixed up with his own sentences, such as Happy is he that taketh Thy little ones and dasheth their heads against the stones."

RELIGIOUS PSYCHOSIS

Fish claimed that God had ordered him to torment and castrate little boys. He had actually done so a number of times. What amazed and shocked Wertham the most was when Fish described the cannibalism he inflicted on the body of young Billy Gaffney: "His state of mind while he described these things in minute detail was a peculiar mixture. He spoke in a matter-of-fact way, like a housewife describing her favorite methods of cooking... But at times his voice and facial expression indicated a kind of satisfaction and ecstatic thrill. I said to myself: However you define the medical and legal borders of sanity, this certainly is beyond that border." Wertham had no problem in confirming that Albert Fish was suffering from a religious psychosis. There was little doubt about that. It could be corroborated by his children who had observed him hitting himself on his nude body with a nail-studded paddle until he was covered with blood. They also saw him stand alone on a hill with his hands raised, shouting at the top of his voice: "I am Christ."

At one stage Fish told the psychiatrist: "What I did must have been right or an angel would have stopped me, just as an angel stopped Abraham in the Bible from sacrificing his son."

Wertham had no problem giving his expert opinion that the accused, his patient, Albert Fish was legally insane: "I characterized his personality as introverted and extremely infantilistic... I outlined his abnormal mental make-up, and his mental disease, which I diagnosed as paranoid psychosis... Because Fish suffered from delusions and particularly was so mixed up about the questions of punishment, sin, atonement, religion, torture, self-punishment, he had a perverted, a distorted, if you want, an insane, knowledge of right and wrong. His test was that if it had been wrong he would have been stopped, as Abraham was stopped, by an angel."

But it was an admission made by Fish and later retold to Dempsey that ultimately convinced Wertham that Fish was unfit to face trial.

Fish told him that after he had decapitated Grace Budd he tried to drink her blood which had spilled into the paint can he had placed underneath her head to catch it. The blood was warm and it made him choke so he stopped drinking it after three or four swallows. He then took his sharp butcher's knife and began slicing pieces of flesh from her body and, in particular, her breast, buttocks and abdomen. He then chopped off her ears and nose. He wrapped the body parts in a piece of old newspaper and carried them back to his rooms. Simply by holding this package on his lap as he rode the train home gave him such a sexual high that caused him to spontaneously ejaculate.

As soon as he got back to his rooms he cut the child's flesh into smaller pieces and used them to make a stew which he infused with carrots, onions and strips of bacon. He stretched the stew out to last nine days to enhance the pleasure as long as he could. During all of this time he had retained a state of sexual heaven which necessitated him to masturbate several times a day. He would savor the food at night while he lay awake in the darkness and masturbate himself to sleep. Then as soon as he awoke the following day the sexual arousal would begin again.

2. HENRY HOWARD HOLMES (1861-1896)

"I was born with the devil in me. I could not help the fact that I was a murderer no more than a poet can help the inspiration to sing....I was born with the Evil One standing as my sponsor beside the bed where I was ushered into the world, and he has been with me ever since."

– H. H. Holmes

Dr. Henry Howard Holmes is one of the America's first documented serial killers in the modern sense of the word. The ultimate lady killer, Holmes is credited with a confirmed kill count of twenty seven but it is generally accepted that his real body count was well over one hundred. Recent evidence, physical and forensic, which was uncovered in 2013, suggests that there is a growing likelihood that he may also have been the infamous Jack the Ripper. This is his story.

Dr. Holmes was actually born Herman Webster Mudgett on the 16 May 1861 in Gilmanton, New Hampshire to Levi Horton Mudgett and his wife, Theodate Page Price. Both his parents were descendants from the first European settlers in the area. His father was from farming stock and he himself was a decent, hard-working farmer, a devout Methodist and a violent alcoholic. His family were well to do and Herman enjoyed a privileged upbringing.

He was a quiet and insular child, slightly built with brown hair and piercing blue eyes. Herman was frequently the subject of his father's wrath and was severely punished for any wrongdoing. His mother, a pious and submissive woman, left such matters as discipline to her beloved husband, Levi. Herman hated both his parents and longed for the day he was old enough to leave Gilmanton.

Fortunately, he was a bright student, much smarter than his peers but this too had its disadvantages. He was frequently bullied at school and often made the butt of practical jokes. His fascination with life and death and dead bodies probably began as a result of one of these practical jokes. He was five and was in his first year at school. The local doctor's house was on his way to school and Herman believed the stories the older boys told him that the doctor's house was full of body parts including human heads in glass jars. Herman made sure to quicken his step every time he passed the house.

Once the older boys realized his fear of the house they hijacked him one day and dragged him screaming and kicking in the "house of horrors." This traumatic incident was to have a profound effect on Herman. It terrified him but it also intrigued him. It was at that very moment that he decided that he too would, one day, become a doctor. By the age of eleven Herman was already conducting his own medical experiments on animals. He would catch, kill and dissect any stray animals he could find. Later he began to experiment on the animals while they were still alive, dissecting certain parts of their limbs and organs to determine how long they would survive without them.

Not much is known about his life until July 1878 when on Independence Day, at the age of just seventeen, Herman Mudgett married Clara Lovering in Alton, New Hampshire. Their son, Robert, was born on the 3 February, 1880 in Loudon, New Hampshire. Mudgett attended Michigan Medical School and thus began his life of crime. Here, while studying to become a doctor, Mudgett is known to have stolen dead bodies from the laboratory in order to carry out insurance scams. These scams provided him with sufficient money to move to the Windy City and set up his own business in the related field of pharmaceuticals. It was, at this time, and probably calculated to avoid detection in the insurance scams he had committed, that Mudgett decided to change his name to Dr. Henry Howard Holmes.

Holmes, as he was now called, had been a frequent visitor to Chicago. The city had recently been rebuilt following a devastating fire which had destroyed most of its wooden buildings. In 1886 he secured a position as a druggist in the pharmacy of E. S. Holston in the Chicago suburb of Englewood. Within a year he had swindled the owners out of the profitable store and murdered the proprietor's widow.

An ordinary decent fraudster might have been satisfied but Holmes was no ordinary decent fraudster; he was a serial fraudster who was prepared to kill to achieve his ambitions. Holmes only ever viewed the Holston Drugstore as a means to an end. He had no interest in drugs, indeed no interest in medicine. His sole purpose in life was to make money, lots of it, and he determined that nothing would stop him making it.

On a business trip to Minneapolis in December 1886, Holmes met and fell in love with a young lady by the name of Myrta Z. Belknap and following a whirlwind romance, the happy couple exchanged vows in Minneapolis on the 28 January 1887 before returning to Chicago. Myrta worked in the drugstore alongside her newly wedded husband and everything went swimmingly, at least, for the first few months. Because she cramped his style, she was then dispatched upstairs to carry out whatever few household duties needed to be taken care of. Eventually the marriage broke down and Myrta moved out with their only child to a modest house in Wilmette just north of Chicago. Somewhat surprisingly, but probably to avoid a scandal, Holmes agreed to pay her weekly maintenance and for the first time in his life resolved to continue the payments. But more than likely it was because Holmes would have been revealed as a bigamist had he not maintained her.

With Myrta out of the way, Holmes began the first part of his master plan. He first secured a lease on the vacant lot that lay directly across the road from his drugstore. The lease was signed in the summer of 1888 and then for several months Holmes disappeared. In a recent, somewhat sensational article, the *Chicago Tribune* suggest that Dr. Holmes took a trip abroad and arrived in London in late summer 1888.

At that very time, it can only be of the utmost coincidence, that five prostitutes were butchered in the back alleys of London's notoriously squalid East End by a person unknown who was subsequently given the name *Jack the Ripper*. For the purposes of our story the dates of the killings are of particular interest. Mary Anne Nicholls was murdered on the 31 August, 1888. Her body was found at Buck's Row. The second killing, of Annie Chapman, took place a week later on the 8 September at the rear of 29 Hanbury Street. Both bodies had been horribly mutilated with a knife by a person believed or suspected to have had surgical experience.

On the 28 September the Metropolitan Police received a letter, purporting to be from the killer. It was signed "Jack the Ripper." On the 16 October a second letter was sent to George Lusk, head of the Whitechapel Vigilance Committee. The letter read: "Sir I send you half the kidne I took from one woman prasarved it for you tother piece I fried and ate it it was very nise I may send you the bloody knife that I took it out if you only wate a whit longer. Signed Catch me when you can Mister Lusk." The top of the letter had the words "From Hell" written on the upper right hand corner.

The letter did indeed enclose part of a human kidney. Three further murders took place between the 30 September and the 9 November. And then they suddenly stopped. No one was ever caught for the killings and only recently has Dr. Holmes been mentioned as a possible suspect.

Holmes resurfaced in Chicago in the Fall of 1888 and began construction on what was later to be called the Murder Castle. The Murder Castle was his grand plan. It was a development with retail shops and hotel accommodation. It took almost two years to build but should have taken less than a year. The main reason for the delay in building the Castle was that Holmes never had the money to complete it.

The secondary reason was that he never wanted anyone to work on it long enough to know the actual interior design. Accordingly, it was quite usual for workers to be dismissed every two weeks. No one ever lasted in the job more than a month. No one would ever be able to reveal the secrets that lurked within.

The ground floor consisted of a number of retail shops. Some of these shops were rented to outside tenants while others were operated by Holmes himself. It was from the second and third floors that the hotel business was operated. The second floor has been described as maze-like and "its floor plan was similar to the labyrinthine layout of a carnival funhouse."

There were fifty one doors in six narrow corridors behind which lay thirty five rooms, many of which were bedrooms. Some of the other rooms were airtight, lined with asbestos-covered steel plates; others were more like closets, very narrow and with low ceilings. Some of the rooms were soundproofed. Holmes called them ancillary rooms. But ancillary to what? The top floor consisted of Holmes's private office which overlooked Wallace Street, and thirty six guest rooms which were unexceptionally furnished with beds, rugs, bureaux, wall mirrors and chairs which one would expect to find in an establishment of this type at the time. The most obvious strangeness about the design was the corridors. They were narrow, dimly lit, and zig-zagged at weird angles.

Those rooms which were open to paying guests, seemed to be normal conventional bedrooms but they weren't. Most of the rooms were fitted with gas pipes connected to a control panel in Holmes' rooms. They were used, not to heat the rooms, but to poison the occupants. Doors could only be locked from the outside. There were concealed peepholes through which Holmes could observe his guests.

The second floor also contained secret passageways, trapdoors, concealed closets and large, greased shafts, wide enough to accommodate human bodies, which ran down to the cellar. The brick walled cellar resembled a set from a Hammer horror movie with grim paraphernalia, an acid tank, quicklime vats, dissecting tables, a surgeon's operating table and medical instruments. There was also a contraption which Holmes called "an elasticity determinator" which was nothing more than a modern day torture rack.

It was obvious from this inventory that Holmes had planned to gas his guests, dispatch them down the chutes and then experiment on them. But Holmes was not a man who killed simply for the thrill of it. Holmes was a man who also murdered for profit and he already had a cunning plan up his sleeve. Having murdered his victims, Holmes intended skinning them and selling their skeletons to medical schools. Meanwhile to help finance the completion of the Castle, Holmes was obliged to sell his original pharmacy. Immediately afterwards he opened a new pharmacy across the street.

Holmes enjoyed many mistresses but one in particular is worth mentioning. Her name was Julia Smythe and she was from Davenport. She was also the wife of Icilius T. Conner, one of his commercial tenants. Holmes seduced her and she moved in with him. When she came to know too much of his business he murdered her.

A secretive and cautious man like Holmes has few if any friends but nearly always must rely on someone as a right hand man. Sometime in 1889, Benjamin Freelon Pitezel, a confirmed alcoholic with a string of convictions for petty crimes like larceny and forgery, became Dr. Holmes' right hand man.

It was Pitezel who introduced the randy doctor to the delicious Emeline Cigrand, a tall and beautiful blonde from Lafayette, Indiana. He initially employed her as his personal secretary but it was only a matter of months before she became his mistress. She worked for Holmes for only six months but during that time learned too much of his dubious dealings or so Holmes must have thought because sometime in December 1892 he murdered the young lady.

The Chicago World Fair otherwise known as The World's Columbian Exposition was a World's Fair held in Chicago in 1893 to celebrate the 400th anniversary of Christopher Columbus' arrival in the New World in 1492. The Fair attracted in excess of twenty seven million visitors during its six month tenure. All of these visitors needed somewhere to stay. Accommodation in Chicago was in short supply and Holmes with his new hotel knew he would make a killing.

No one know for certain just how many of these visitors were lured to their death by the evil Dr. Holmes in his Castle of Horrors but the indications are that the Castle was fully booked on most nights. Holmes concentrated mostly on women, particularly women travelling alone.

Most of these were gassed, dispatched down the greased chutes and dismembered in the basement before suffering one of two fates. They would either be burned in the giant kiln or their skeletal remains would be sold to medical schools across America. Thus, Holmes was not just able to rob them of their possessions but in many cases profit from their remains.

Holmes fell in love with many women during his life; the greater the fortune, the greater the love. Certainly this was so in the seduction of Miss Minnie Williams. He met Minnie in March 1893. She began as his private secretary and quickly graduated to his mistress and then fiancée. It may have surprised some because Minnie was short and plump and very different to his other conquests. But what she lacked in looks she made up for in inheritance. Minnie was the heir to a considerable fortune; $40,000 to be precise.

It was a sum that would get him out of debt. Despite appearances, Holmes was hopelessly bankrupt. It was only a matter of time before his creditors would seize all his assets, including the clothes on his back. The country's economy had faltered and by 1893 a number of his creditors had joined forces and were closing in on him.

Holmes had persuaded the ever gullible Minnie to transfer her real estate assets into his name but now he needed to liquidate them to get his hands on the cash. But there were two obstacles he had encountered. One was the location of her property. It was in Fort Worth, several hundred miles away. The second was the increasing interference of Minnies' sister, Nannie. Holmes eventually murdered both Minnie and Nannie.

He still had not managed to satisfy his creditor's claims. He had made up his mind, the Castle would have to go. But first he needed to secure adequate fire insurance. He proceeded to take out insurance totaling $25,000 with four separate insurance companies. When the third floor of the building mysterious burst into flames in October of that year the fire brigade were called and performed such an excellent job that they managed to save the ground and first floors. Holmes was furious but, in any event, he set about making his claim. But the insurance company refused to pay. Holmes was determined that they wouldn't best him and began the implementation of yet another audacious plan.

The plan involved his loyal lieutenant Ben Pitezel. The plan itself was simple. Holmes would take out a large life insurance policy on the life of Pitezel. They would stage an accident as a result of which the police would find Pitezel's dead body. Only it wouldn't be Pitezel's body. It would be someone else and they would so disfigure the corpse as to make proper identification impossible to anyone other than Holmes. This would necessitate Pitezel going into hiding but other than that the plan should work a treat. Once he collected on the policy Holmes agreed to split the proceeds.

The problem with most serial killers, and Holmes is no exception, is that they are pathological liars. They are simply incapable of telling even the simplest truth and accordingly can never be trusted. But Pitezel trusted Holmes and on the 9 November 1893 Ben Pitezel's life was insured for $10,000 by the Fidelity Mutual Life Association.

As his creditors were about to pounce, Holmes decided it was more prudent to get out of Chicago for the last time. But first he married Georgina Yoke on the 9 January 1894 in Denver, Colorado. The certificate certified that Miss Georgiana Yoke had married one Henry Mansfield Howard. It took him a year to tell her the truth about his real financial circumstances. In the end she accepted it. What else could she do? The pair travelled to Fort Worth where they met up with Mr. Pitezel. Here, the two desperadoes engaged in a large number of scams which netted them close to $20,000. It was more than enough for their purposes but enough was never enough for redoubtable H.H. Holmes.

He then became involved in a ridiculous scheme involving the larceny of horses and for the first time in his life, Holmes was caught out before the scam was completed. The trio fled Fort Worth in the middle of the night. But Texans take horse theft very seriously and they had no intention of allowing them get away with it. The next stop was St. Louis where Holmes decided to re-enact one of his first swindles that had worked so well for him. He sought out and found the owner of a drugstore that was in the market for a sale. With a small down payment he acquired the premises.

He then used the stores credit to acquire a huge amount of stock from the Merrill Drug Company. Having acquired the stock he promptly sold it off. He then sold the drugstore with a phony bill of sale. He had calculated that by the time the fraud was unraveled he would be far away from St. Louis. However, the drug company immediately reported the fraud to the police. Holmes was arrested and jailed for fraud. Despite a lifetime of murder, larceny and theft this was the only time Holmes had ever seen the inside of a jail cell. It should have been a chastening experience. It wasn't.

When he was bailed out just ten days later by his wife he informed his lieutenant Pitezel he had met someone inside and that the meeting was wonderfully fortuitous. The man he had met was train robber Marion Hedgepeth. Holmes had told him all about his proposed insurance scam and Hedgepeth, for a share of the spoils, had given him the name of a crooked lawyer to help him collect the money.

At the time of Holmes' arrest, Pitezel had been joined by his wife Carrie and their five children, Dessie, Alice, Nellie, Howard and baby Wharton. Carrie was none too impressed when her husband outlined the insurance scam he and Holmes intended to pull off for a bounty of $10,000. She demanded to know where was all the money he had already made in Fort Worth? Holmes was looking after it for him. When he promised that this would be his very last dodgy deal and he would never associate with Holmes again she very reluctantly agreed to allow him continue. She was to be named as sole beneficiary.

They had decided that the phony death would take place somewhere in Philadelphia where the Fidelity Life Assurance Association had its head office. When they arrived in Philadelphia they set about their two main tasks; finding a suitable location to stage the death and finding a suitable cadaver to substitute for Pitezel's body. They found the former at 1316 Callowhill Street but the latter proved somewhat more difficult to find. Eventually, as Pitezel and Holmes drank coffee in a restaurant one day, Holmes got a call from a former associate in New York City. They had their cadaver. But Holmes, as he eyed up his lieutenant, Benjamin Franklon Pitezel, knew he never really needed a cadaver at all.

When Marion Hedgepeth opened his daily edition of the *St. Louis Globe Democrat* he read about the unfortunate death by burning in Philadelphia, he jumped for joy. He never believed that his old cell mate would go through with his crazy insurance scam. But he had, and now Marion was looking forward to the check for $500 that Holmes had promised to send him once the job was done. No one will ever know what would have happened if Holmes had kept his side of the bargain but when he didn't Hedgepeth wrote a very long and revealing letter to the Fidelity Life Assurance Association. He told them of a scam which involved insuring a man named Benjamin Pitezel for $10,000 and then faking his death in a laboratory explosion by substituting a cadaver.

The protagonist was a gentleman by the name of H. H. Howard. Hedgepeth's sole involvement was to collect $500 for introducing him to a shyster lawyer. But Howard (Holmes) had reneged on the deal and had fled with the proceeds. The Fidelity Life soon realized that H.M. Howard was none other than the incorrigible H. H. Holmes, lately of Chicago.

The company re-opened their file and re-examined the circumstances surrounding the discovery of a body at 1316 Callowhill Street in Philadelphia. The body had been discovered in a state of rigor mortis and was so badly burned in the face from chemicals and sun exposure that identity of the person was impossible. Nevertheless, H. H. Holmes, who, at the time, was accompanied by one of Benjamin Pitezel's children, had indeed identified this body. From certain characteristics they certified the remains as those of Pitezel.

Once Holmes had received the money, through the shyster lawyer, he had vanished and had taken the Pitezel's children with him. Unable to locate him, they engaged the services of detectives from the Pinkerton National Detective Agency. They followed his trail around the country.

The more they traveled, the more they became aware of his multitude of frauds, thefts, and schemes, including other insurance scams years earlier in Chicago that had enabled him with sufficient funds to build the Castle hotel. They regarded him as one of the top fraudsters they had ever come across. But these were experienced detectives and they were soon to close the net on the elusive H. H. Holmes.

When it was discovered that Holmes had killed three of the children he was caught and charged with murder. They tracked him down in Vermont and kept him under surveillance until they arranged for his arrest on the 16 November, 1894 as Holmes boarded a steamship on his way out of the country. Holmes eventually confessed.

On the 12 September Holmes was indicted for the murder of Benjamin Pitezel. He entered a plea of not guilty and his trial date was scheduled for the 28 October. In a pathetic attempt to explain his life of crime and against the wishes of his lawyers, Holmes, who was now only thirty four, wrote a book called Holmes' Own Story, in which the Alleged Multimurderer and Arch Conspirator Tells of the Twenty-two Tragic Deaths and Disappearances in which he is Said to be Implicated. No one took this drivel seriously and his trial which began on the 28 October, lasted just five days.

The jury had heard enough. They convicted Holmes of the murder of Benjamin Pitezel. Judge Arnold sentenced him to death by hanging. After his conviction, and as his attorneys prepared an appeal for a new trial, which was unsuccessful, Holmes wrote yet another account of his life for which he was paid $10,000 by the Hearst newspaper syndicate. It was published in *The Philadelphia Inquirer*. He now claimed to have murdered over one hundred people but he later amended this to twenty seven. It seemed as if he would pluck the figures out of thin air. On May 7, 1896, Holmes was hanged at Moyamensing Prison, in Philadelphia. When his neck did not properly snap he was slowly strangled to death and pronounced dead after twenty minutes of strangulation.

MAD OR BAD

The criminological theories at the time were fueled by Cesare Lombroso, an Italian anthropologist and professor at the University of Turin. By 1876, Lombroso had published his famous work, *L'uomo delinquente*.

Believing that human behavior could be classified with objective tests, Lombroso was convinced that certain people were born criminals, identifiable by specific physical traits, such as bulging brows, long arms, and ape-like noses. They were throwbacks to more primitive times, and he called them degenerates. Lombroso's theories had spread quickly across Europe and America, supported by the new evolutionary thinking.

Holmes believed the theories and tried to use them for his own advantage. In another decade or so, Lombroso would be largely discredited. Yet, in keeping with the theory, Holmes "saw" a prominence on one side of his head and a "corresponding diminution on the other side." Also, a deficiency on his nose and ear, and the lengthening or shortening of various limbs.

Holmes said he was confessing in part to justify the scientific deductions. Little did he know they weren't scientific at all. But his motive was more likely to bring attention to himself and to wallow in one last flight of grandiosity. No doubt he enjoyed the idea of having an audience. Holmes' attorneys had turned down an offer of $5,000 for his body, and even refused his brain to

Philadelphia's Wistar Institute, which hoped to have its experts analyze the organ for better understanding of the criminal mind.

During this case, another American phenomenon arose from society's fascination with sensational crime. Thousands of people lined up to see the Chicago murder site, so a former police officer remodeled the infamous building as "Holmes's Horror Castle," an attraction that offered guided tours to the suffocation chambers and torture rooms. But before it opened it mysteriously burned to the ground.

So many people who'd rented rooms from Holmes during the fair had actually gone missing that sensational estimates of his victims reached around two hundred, and some people perpetuated this unsubstantiated toll even today.

It's likely that Holmes' own figure from his recanted confession is low, but there is no way to know just how many he actually killed. A record of his many other frauds can be found in the authors noted in the bibliography

WAS H.H.HOLMES ACTUALLY JACK THE RIPPER?

In 2013 the *Chicago Sun Times* and the *British Daily Mail* published articles that a gentleman by the name of Jeff Mudgett had submitted handwriting samples from both H. H. Holmes and *Jack the Ripper* for review and handwriting experts had confirmed the likelihood they could stem from the same hand.

Jeff Mudgett, who has written an intriguing book called Bloodstains, is the great great grandson of H. H. Holmes so his revelations cannot be so easily dismissed. In fact, there are several reasons which suggest that Homes was Jack the Ripper. The first of these is that the Ripper murders were committed in late 1888s. Despite the fact that Holmes' life is well documented by such illustrious authors as H.B. Irvine, Pinkerton and Schechter, none of these fine men can account for Holmes during that period. He seems to have disappeared out of Chicago for several weeks. So, where was he at that time? Is it possible that he travelled to England in the fall of 1888?

On the 31 August, 1888, the body of Mary Ann Nichols was found butchered on the streets of Whitechapel. Her body was mutilated, with one gash reaching from the pelvis to the breastbone. A week later, Annie Chapman became the second victim of *Jack the Ripper*. She was so badly mutilated that her head was almost completely severed. Her body was literally ripped apart, and her viscera scattered around her body in a grotesque display.

Three weeks later, the Ripper attacked not one but two victims in the same night in what became known as the "double event." The murder of Elizabeth Stride, was the least brutal. Her throat was slit but unlike the previous two victims her body was not heavily mutilated probably because her attacker was interrupted. Within three hours, Catherine Eddowes was viciously attacked and her body was disemboweled. Furthermore, her throat was slit and her nose almost completely severed off. Her lungs were thrown aside, with her entrails twisted into the gaping wound around the neck.

The Ripper's final victim was Mary Jane Kelly whose body was found in her room on the 9 November, 1888. Her death was described by the New York Times as follows: "The most terrible wholesale mutilation it is possible to imagine. Her head was severed and placed between one of her arms. Her ears and nose had been cut off. The body had been disemboweled and the flesh was torn from the thighs. Several organs were missing. The skin had been torn off of the forehead and cheeks. The victim's breast and viscera were removed and lying on a table. One of the victim's hands had been pushed into the stomach."

This was the only one of the Ripper murders to have been committed inside. Is it possible that the Ripper realized the benefits of time and security when the crime takes place indoors? Is that why he immediately returned to Chicago to oversee construction of the Castle, stockpiled as it was with surgical equipment and torture devices with which he could indulge his heinous crimes for hours on end within the privacy of his own home?

Furthermore, it is believed that the Ripper murders were carried out by someone with surgical experience. Dr. George Baxter Phillips, observed that the wounds on Annie Chapman's body were: "made by a sharp knife with a narrow blade and that the evisceration indicated some medical knowledge." Holmes had graduated from the University of Michigan's Medical School and enjoyed extensive surgical ability.

Another interesting note is that due to the wounds on the bodies, it has been suggested that the Ripper was left handed. So was Holmes.

The Ripper murders occurred during a very short period of time beginning in late 1888s and then suddenly stopped. By the time they had stopped, Holmes was back in Chicago giving instructions for the construction of his Castle hotel and its torture chamber where he was soon to begin his mutilation and dissection of his female victims.

During this period of time, someone who called himself *Jack the Ripper*, wrote two letters. One letter was sent to the Press and one letter which included part of a human kidney was received by George Lusk of the Whitechapel

Vigilance Committee. Jeff Mudgett claims that he has had letters written by his great great grandfather H. H. Holmes when in prison compared to letters supposedly written by *Jack the Ripper* and the writing in them is identical. But more of this later.

The Ripper sent his first letter on the 25 September 1888. It began, "Dear Boss." It ended "Your truly." Both phrases were Americanisms. British people began their letter with "Dear Sir" and ended them with either "Yours sincerely or Your faithfully."

The second letter, sent to George Lusk, was sent on the 15 October 1888. Across the top of the letter the words "From Hell" were written. Holmes was obsessed with hell and in his own confession wrote: "I was born with the Devil in me. I could not help the fact that I was a murderer, no more than the poet can help the inspiration to sing ... I was born with the Evil One standing as my sponsor beside the bed where I was ushered into this world, and he has been with me since."

It is a well-known fact that each of the Ripper's victims was mutilated worse than the previous leading up to the almost complete dissection of Mary Jane Kelly within the confines of her own room. Is it merely coincidence then, that just after the Ripper vanishes from the streets of London, that Holmes begins dissecting his victims is his personally designed Murder Castle?

According to what is known as the "depression phase theory", Holmes' first victims would be the natural step up from the Ripper's last. Allow me to give a brief explanation of the term "depression phase theory." Serial killing is said to contain seven separate and distinct phases; the Aura Phase, the Trolling Phase, the Wooing Phase, the Capture Phase, the Murder Phase, the Totem Phase, and finally, the Depression Phase. The Depression Phase is the most important phase to explore in the case of the Ripper and Holmes as it takes place after the crime, when the killer has come down from his emotional high. In this phase he experiences a feeling of hopelessness and lack of fulfillment.

This then causes a succession of increasingly violent acts as the cycle of phases repeats itself. Within the confines and safety of the basement of his Murder Castle did Dr. H. H. Holmes carry out even more atrocious mutilations than before?

Accepting that the above arguments are circumstantial let us now examine the more scientific evidence. This relates to forensic tests carried out on the handwriting contained in the Ripper letters and Holmes's handwriting as well as the description and physical attributes of both men.

In his book Bloodstains published in 2011 Jeff Mudgett outlines the forensic tests carried out on both sets of handwriting. He submitted handwriting evidence to the British Library who after their own review recommended that he send the material to Ms. Margaret Webb for a professional expert opinion. They said that she could determine if the letters from the Ripper and from Holmes were written by the same hand.

Following an examination, Ms. Webb concluded that both were absolutely from the same hand, and that Holmes was the author of the Ripper letters.

However, when her opinion was released, she was, not surprisingly, attacked by a number of scholars. The principle reason for the attack was not so much directed at her integrity but more at the fact that she was a graphologist and not solely a handwriting expert.

Mr. Mudgett then sought out another expert. He was aware the U.S. Post Office and Department of Justice had hired a mathematical and scientific firm at the University of Buffalo to create a computer program to differentiate the millions of styles of handwriting.

The firm was led by Dr. Sargur Srihari and Dr. Venu Govindaraju who had created what was called the Cedar-Fox program. When activated the new program was getting it right 96% of the time. Mudgett asked them if they would test the letters. They agreed.

The conclusion reached by these scientists was that the classifier performance number, which they rated at 97.95%, could "be taken to indicate the JTR [Jack the Ripper] and Mudgett [Holmes] classes are similar in style."

To understand this number, you should know that if you compare two documents written by yourself, the number would never reach 100%. This would seem to indicate that the Ripper letters were written by H. H. Holmes. And what of the similar physical characteristics?

In 2006 Scotland Yard together with the BBC created a computer composite of *Jack the Ripper* based on the thirteen eyewitness accounts from 1888 statements. The computer composite was superimposed on the photograph of H. H. Holmes and was a 100% perfect match!

Finally, most scholars agree that serial killers continue through their cycle of killing until one of two possible situations occur. They die or they get caught. They do not suddenly decide, enough is enough, it's time to retire. Sometimes a serial killer will stop suddenly, only to recommence just as suddenly, sometime later. In such circumstances, the killer has usually been incarcerated for an unrelated offense. The British killer Fred West, the

German killer Peter Kurten, the American killer John Wayne Gacy are just three of many examples of serial killers who stopped and resumed after their release from prison.

The only other reason that a serial killer would break the cycle is if he dies. The Ripper was never caught but his killing spree ended very suddenly and never recommenced, at least not in London. Did *Jack the Ripper* recommence his killings in the Chicago suburb of Englewood? Holmes was executed in May 1896, after which neither he nor Jack was ever heard from again. Was H.H. Holmes actually *Jack the Ripper*? You decide.

3. THEORDORE ROBERT BUNDY (1946-1989)

"I'm as cold a motherfucker as you've ever put your fucking eyes on. I don't give a shit about those people"

– Ted Bundy

Theodore Robert Cowell had the ability, personality and ambition to become Governor of the State of Washington for the Republican Party. Instead, he chose to become America's most notorious serial killer. After decades of denial, he confessed on his deathbed to thirty murders but some commentators have claimed that the total could be as high as one hundred. Like many serial killers, Bundy was a pathological liar so it was impossible to believe anything he said.

This is probably the reason why the various books written about him can be contradictory in detailing various parts of his life. He would give one explanation to one biographer and a different explanation to another. He was executed by electric chair at Florida State Prison, Bradford County, Florida on the 24 January 1989 aged just forty two.

"Ted was the very definition of heartless evil." – Defense Attorney Polly Nelson

Theodore Robert Cowell was born to Eleanor Louise Cowell at the Lund Family Center in Burlington Vermont on the 24 November 1946.

He was born to Eleanor Louise Cowell in Burlington Vermont on the 24 November 1946. He never knew his father. Until the age of three, he lived in the Philadelphia home of his maternal grandparents, Samuel and Eleanor Cowell whom he believed were his parents. They told him that his mother was actually his sister. In 1950 his mother changed her surname from Cowell to Nelson and dropped her first name Eleanor. She left Philadelphia with Ted to live with her cousins. A year later she met and fell in love with Johnny Culpepper Bundy and married within a year. Johnny Bundy formally adopted Ted but it always remained a difficult relationship. Throughout his entire life Bundy was a pathological liar and a kleptomaniac who would steal anything that wasn't nailed down.

As a young man Bundy appears to have been unfocussed as regards his future. In 1965, after graduating from high school, he attended the University of Puget Sound (UPS) but only stayed a year before transferring to the University of Washington (UW) to study Chinese. In 1967 he fell in love with a beautiful girl from a wealthy family called Stephanie Brooks. Bundy was devastated when she broke off the relationship. His life then went downhill. In early 1968 Bundy dropped out of college and worked at a series of minimum-wage jobs. He travelled to Colorado and then further east, visiting relatives in Arkansas and Philadelphia. He then enrolled for one semester at Temple University.

Later he re-enrolled in the University of Washington and began studying psychology, at which he excelled. It was as if the new Ted Bundy was driven to prove his worth. Back in Washington, towards the end of 1969, he met Elizabeth Kloepfer sometimes identified in biographies as Meg Anders, Beth Archer, or Liz Kendall. She was a divorcée from Ogden, Utah who worked as a secretary at the University of Washington, School of Medicine. They were to spend the next five years in an on-off relationship.

Bundy graduated from the University of Washington in 1974 and became involved in politics. In 1973, during a trip to California on Republican Party business, Bundy met up again with Stephanie Brooks. She was amazed at the transformation in him. They began dating again and when she fell for him and thought they would marry he callously dumped her without a word of explanation.

No one knows for certain when Ted Bundy began killing beautiful young women but it was definitely as early as 1969 and maybe even 1961. He began killing in earnest in 1974. Most of his victims were young, white, beautiful women with long brown hair. His *modus operandi* was that he would pretend to be injured and ask them for assistance. He lured them to his car, abducted them and brought them to a place to torture them. He raped them before killing and would often return to have sex with the corpse.

He began his first killing campaign in Washington, Oregon. College students went missing at the rate of one per month. The Pacific Northwest murders culminated on the 14 July 1974 with the broad-daylight abductions of two women from a crowded beach at Lake Sammamish State Park in Issaquah, twenty miles east of Seattle.

In August 1974 Bundy was accepted into the University of Utah Law School. He left his girlfriend Elizabeth Kloepfer behind and moved to Salt Lake City but he couldn't cope with the study program and was out of his depth. Not long after he arrived in Utah the State experienced a rash of unexplained murders which remained unsolved until his ultimate confession. They all occurred towards the end of 1974. Years later Bundy was to admit that having killed the girls he would return to the crime scene and spend time with his dead victims. Sometimes he would wash their hair. On another occasion he applied make up to one of the victims.

Meanwhile, Elizabeth Kloepfer, having read that young women were disappearing in towns surrounding Salt Lake

City reported him to King County, not once but three times. Bundy's name was eventually added to their list of suspects, but at that time no credible evidence linked him to the Utah crimes. It was during 1975 that Bundy was to move much of his criminal activity eastward to Colorado from his base in Utah. He began in January when on the 12th of that month he abducted and murdered nurse Caryn Campbell, ski instructor Julie Cunningham, Denise Oliverson, and twelve year old Lynette Culver and Susan Curtis. Her murder was Bundy's last confession before he was executed. The bodies of Cunningham, Culver, Curtis, and Oliverson have never been recovered.

He was arrested in August 1975 by a Utah Highway Patrol officer in Salt Lake City for failing to pull over for a routine traffic stop. After searching his apartment he was placed on around the clock surveillance. When Bundy sold his VW beetle in September the Utah police impounded it from its new owner and the FBI dismantled and forensically searched it for incriminating evidence. A previous victim he had abducted and who had escaped was Carole Da Ronch and when she picked him out of a police line-up he was arrested and charged with aggravated kidnapping and attempted criminal assault. It was all they had on him at the time. His parents put up bail of $15,000 and he was released.

There were now three separate investigations into the activities of Ted Bundy; in Utah, Washington and in Colorado. They had him for abduction and assault. They wanted him for murder. The trial for the Da Ronch kidnapping took place in February 1976. The judge, after a four day trial and a weekend of deliberation, found Bundy guilty of kidnapping and assault and sentenced him to one to fifteen years in the Utah State Prison. Then in October the authorities in Colorado charged him with the murder of Caryn Campbell. On the 7 June 1977 he was transported from Garfield County jail to Pitkin County Courthouse in Aspen for a preliminary hearing.

During a recess he escaped but was captured after six days and was returned to Glenwood Springs. He escaped from there on the 30 December. He was already in Chicago before the authorities realized he was gone. Bundy's ultimate destination was Florida and he arrived in Tallahassee on the 8 January 1978. He changed his name to Chris Hagen and went on the rampage again. On a single night he broke into a house on a university campus and severely beat up four female students killing two of them, Lisa Levy and Margaret Bowman. Referred to as the Chi Omega Murders this fifteen minutes of mayhem produced a witness, Nita Neary, who saw Bundy run from the building. He then attacked another student Cheryl Thomas eight blocks away. He had only been in Tallahasse seven days.

One month later, Bundy stole a white van and drove to Jacksonville where he targeted fourteen year old Leslie Parmenter, but was unsuccessful. Her father, Detective James Parmenter, wasted no time in trying to track him down. Now out of control, he drove to Lake City the following day where he murdered twelve year old Kimberly Diane Leach. On the 12 February he stole a car and drove to Alabama but was stopped for a routine check by Pensacola police officer David Lee who, on discovering the car was stolen, arrested him. As police held Bundy in custody they began the process of collecting critical evidence to be used against him in the murder of Kimberly Leach. He was soon charged with her murder. Later he was also charged with the two Chi Omega Murders.

Bundy's trial for the Chi Omega Murders and assaults was fixed for June 1979 following a change of venue to Miami. The trial was one of the biggest America had ever seen and was the first to be televised live. It attracted over 250 journalists from all over the world. In the end, on the 24 July 1979, after deliberating for seven hours, the jury convicted him of the two murders, three counts of attempted first degree murder, and two counts of burglary. The trial judge imposed death sentences for the murder convictions.

Six months later, after several delays, a second trial took place at the Orange County Courthouse in Orlando for the abduction and murder of Kimberly Leach. Bundy decided to represent himself. The trial took exactly one month. On the 7 February, after less than seven hours of deliberation, the jury returned the verdict finding Bundy guilty on all counts. The sentencing trial began two days later when Bundy shocked those in the courtroom. While interviewing defense witness Carole Ann Boone the two caught everyone off guard when they exchanged vows to marry which under Florida law was enough to seal the marriage contract. Shortly thereafter, the groom was sentenced to death in the electric chair and dispatched to serve his honeymoon alone in a suite on Death Row in Florida State's Raiford Penitentiary. Despite this, in October 1982, Boone gave birth to a daughter and Ted Bundy was named on the birth certificate as the biological father.

Immediately thereafter, Bundy began a long series of appeals all of which failed. In his eleventh hour, he decided to confess to more crimes with a now official death count of thirty six.

Both Ann Rule and Dr. Bob Keppel who both wrote extensively about Bundy, believe that Bundy was likely responsible for the deaths of at least a hundred women, discounting the official count of thirty six victims. Whatever the figure, the fact is no one will ever know for certain how many young innocent women actually fell victim to Ted Bundy.

Bundy declined the offer of a special last meal, so he was given (but did not eat) the traditional steak (medium-rare), eggs (over-easy), hash browns, toast, milk, coffee, juice, butter, and jelly. He was finally executed in the electric chair on the 24 January 1989 at 7:00 a.m.

MAD OR BAD

Was he insane?

The two doctors hired by the State in the appeal cases to evaluate the mental health of Ted Bundy were Charles Mutter and Umesh Mahtre. It is important to point out that they never personally interviewed Bundy. They made diagnoses based solely on written material. Both concluded that Bundy was competent.

The defense also hired a psychologist to evaluate his sanity. Dr. Norman's evaluation surprised the defense team. In his opinion, Bundy murdered girls not because of a mental illness, but because of a simple desire to kill. Bundy never spent any time in a mental home. The question remains, had Ted Bundy been tried in England would he have been found guilty but insane?

In Florida a defendant is only considered to be incompetent to stand trial if he lacks enough rational and factual understanding to co-operate with his lawyer and to understand the charges against him. An evidentiary hearing to determine competency is only allowed if there is clear evidence of substantial doubt about whether the defendant meets those standards. The burden of proof falls on the defense to prove this. Like England and Ireland, the Florida courts recognize and adopt the McNaghten Rules.

If the defendant is unaware that his actions are wrong due to mental illness, or if the defendant is unaware as to what he is doing or of the nature of his actions, then, in those circumstances he is considered legally insane.

Florida law unlike the English common law does not allow a defense of diminished responsibility. The concept of diminished responsibility only applies insofar as it affects the defendant's ability to know right from wrong. Neither does Florida law allow a defense of irresistible impulse which classifies a defendant insane as long as he lacks the ability to control his actions, even if he knows his actions are wrong. Bundy's biggest hurdle in pleading a defense of insanity was that he himself insisted he was sane.

Had the defense of diminished responsibility been open to Bundy to plead and had he allowed it to be used I have no doubt that Ted Bundy would never have been executed. It is somewhat unusual that although Bundy underwent multiple psychiatric examinations the experts' conclusions varied considerably. Dorothy Otnow Lewis a Professor of Psychiatry at the New York University School of Medicine is an authority on violent behavior.

She initially made a diagnosis of bipolar disorder, but later changed her impression more than once. There was some evidence that supported a diagnosis of dissociative identity disorder: A great-aunt witnessed an episode during which Bundy: "... seemed to turn into another, unrecognizable person ... [she] suddenly, inexplicably found herself afraid of her favorite nephew as they waited together at a dusk-darkened train station. He had turned into a stranger."

A prison official in Tallahassee described a similar transformation: "He became weird on me. He did a metamorphosis, a body and facial change, and he felt there was an odor emitting from him…..Almost a complete change of personality ... that was the day I was afraid of him."

There is a general consensus that Bundy suffered from some kind of bipolar disorder or other psychoses, and perhaps an antisocial personality disorder. Sociopaths and psychopaths are known to be outwardly charming, even charismatic; but beneath the facade there is little true personality or genuine insight. Most sociopaths can distinguish right from wrong and are not psychotic, but such ability has minimal effect on their behavior. They do not generally experience feelings of guilt or remorse.

Bundy himself admitted in 1981: "Guilt doesn't solve anything, really. It hurts you. I guess I am in the enviable position of not having to deal with guilt."

4. ED GEIN (1906-1984)

Investigator: "Did you have sexual intercourse with any of the bodies you exhumed?"
Gein: "No, Sir. They smelled too bad."

On the 16 November 1957 Bernice Worden vanished from her hardware shop, the International Harvest Products store in Plainfield, Wisconsin. Mrs. Worden's son, Frank, who was Sheriff Art Schley's deputy, was convinced that a neighbor called Ed Gein was, in some way, involved. Gein had been shopping in his mother's store and said he would return the following morning for a gallon of anti-freeze. Investigators found a sales slip for a gallon of anti-freeze signed by Mrs. Worden on the morning she disappeared. It was the last receipt in the book. Police decided to call upon Gein and arrived at his desolate farmhouse that evening. Gein didn't work the farm, preferring instead to work odd-jobs and take the farm subsidy that was available from the federal government.

On entering the dimly lit farmhouse they noticed he had boarded up rooms previously used by his mother, including the entire upstairs and the parlor and living room downstairs. These rooms were in pristine condition. However, the rest of the house was completely dilapidated. On opening the front door they were overcome by the stench of filth and decomposition. Rubbish, discarded food containers, magazines and papers covered every available surface so much so that it was almost impossible to navigate through the rooms.

They noticed that Gein appeared to be an avid reader of death cult magazines and adventure stories particularly those involving cannibals. Schley decided to check one of the outhouse kitchens with his flashlight. As he moved slowly through the debris he brushed up against something hanging from the ceiling. Shining his torch upwards he noticed a large carcass hanging upside down and dangling from the beams. As it was deer hunting season he assumed the carcass was simply a decapitated and gutted deer. But as he moved closer to inspect it he suddenly realized it was not the carcass of a deer at all. He recoiled in horror as he shone his torch up and down.

No, it wasn't a deer but what the heck was it? It took him a few seconds to realize that what he was looking at was the headless, butchered body of a middle-aged woman. Her wrists were tied with rope and there was a crossbar at her ankles. The torso was "dressed out like a deer." He later discovered that she had been shot with a .22 caliber rifle. The mutilations to her body had been made after death. The body of fifty year old Bernice Worden had been found. But that wasn't the only grisly discovery they would make that day.

As they searched through the rooms of the farmhouse they realized that they had, in fact, stumbled on a body farm. The rooms were decorated with human trophies. The scene was both bizarre and grotesque.

Among the items removed for evidence that day were four human noses, nine masks made from human skin, ten female heads with the tops sawn off, a belt crafted from female human nipples, women's genitalia in a shoebox, ornate bowls made from human skulls, human skulls on his bedposts, a lampshade make from the skin of a human face, a pair of human lips on a drawstring for a window shade and Bernice Worden's head. Police also discovered a second human head in a paper bag.

Ed Gein had a lot of explaining to do about the contents of his house of horrors.

When word got out about what was found on Ed Gein's farm, the news spread like wildfire. News teams from all over America and even further afield descended on the small town of Plainfield, Wisconsin. The town quickly became known worldwide and Ed Gein reached cult status. People were both repulsed and intrigued by the atrocities that took place on Ed Gein's property.

It was a small town and most people knew the Gein family. Despite the fact that he was a little peculiar, sported a quirky grin and had a bizarre sense of humor, neighbors had only good things to say about him; sound, trustworthy and reliable. No one suspected him of being capable of committing such atrocities. But the evidence was there to be seen.

The diminutive, reserved, quiet man the town thought they knew, was in fact, a serial killer and sexual deviant who had also violated the graves of their friends and relatives. It was an open and shut case, or so they first thought.

Ed or Eddie Gein was born Edward Theodore Gein in La Crosse County, Wisconsin on the 27 August 1906 to George and Augusta Gein. He had one brother called Henry who was five years his senior. His mother Augusta Wilhelmine Gein (nee Lehrke) was born in 1878 and was the daughter of Prussian immigrants. She was the major, indeed the sole influence, on his life. Relations between his parents were, to say the least, strained. In fact, Augusta despised her husband and considered him a drunk and good for nothing who couldn't hold down a job. She was right on both counts.

She herself was a fanatically religious woman who when not working in her own grocery store would lecture her boys about the evils of lust and carnal desire. She was determined to raise her sons according to her own strict moral code. She warned them of the dangers of women in general and their looseness and immorality in particular. In her eyes most women were nothing more than prostitutes. Each day she would read to her boys sections from the Bible selecting those verses from the Old Testament that dealt with death, murder and divine resolution.

While their father was timid, Augusta was domineering. She not only controlled the purse strings but also the minds of her family. She sold the store in 1914 and bought an isolated 195 acre farm on the outskirts of the small town of Plainfield and it became the family's permanent home. She wanted to protect her boys from the evils that surrounded them. The nearest neighbors were almost a mile away. But she was unable to isolate her boys completely from the evils of the outside world.

They had to attend school. They were sent to Roche-a-Cri grade school, a tiny building with just twelve students. Ed was an average student who showed no interest in any subject except English. He excelled in reading. He was an effeminate, lonely, small and shy boy and because of this and the fact that he had a lazy eye and a lesion on his tongue which gave him a kind of a lisp, he was frequently bullied.

He became extremely introverted and began to adopt strange mannerisms like random laughing; almost as if he was laughing at himself. Any chance he had of having a normal life was ruined by his mother who discouraged both him and his brother Henry from having any friends.

Although this isolated them and therefore made them unhappy Ed didn't hold it against his mother. In fact, he adored his mother and regarded her as the epitome of everything that was good. For him, she could do no wrong. He never disobeyed her. He also liked his brother and regarded him as a solid, hard-working individual. Tragedy struck in 1940 when their father died from heart failure brought on by his chronic drinking. The death badly affected Henry but had little emotional impact on Ed. To bring in extra cash the two boys undertook odd jobs around the town and this helped support their mother. They were considered trustworthy and reliable by their neighbors.

In fact, Ed often undertook babysitting for many of them. Unlike Henry, Ed never had a girlfriend. He knew his mother wouldn't like him talking to girls and he was completely devoted to his mother. To say he had a mother fixation would be something of an understatement. Henry liked his brother but was concerned that Ed was too attached to his mother. He didn't regard her in the same esteem as Ed and often spoke about her to him in disparaging terms. This sometimes led to friction between the two; a friction that would eventually lead to tragedy.

In May 1944 Henry and Ed were burning waste vegetation on the farm when the fire got out of control threatening the crops and farmhouse. The local fire department were alerted and eventually the fire was extinguished. It was then, at the end of the day, after everyone had left, that Ed reported his brother as missing.

The police were called and Ed, his mother, and two deputies searched the farm for Henry. Although he claimed he had no idea where his brother was, Ed brought them directly to the body. Henry was found lying face down in an area of the farm untouched by the recent fire. He had bruises on his head.

Despite the suspicions of foul play the police dismissed the death as accidental. After all, Ed was a shy, gentle man who wouldn't harm a fly, never mind his own brother, or so they thought. Later, the county coroner officially listed asphyxiation as the cause of death. Ed was now left entirely alone with only his mother as a companion and she wasn't going to be around for very long.

Shortly after Henry's death his mother suffered a paralyzing stroke. Ed devoted his time to looking after her. But following a second stroke her health deteriorated rapidly and she died on the 29 December 1947. Ed was completely devastated by her death.

The farm went to rack and ruin and Ed boarded off most of it, opting to use only the kitchen and a small room off it as a living room and bedroom. This was now his space. He retreated from the real world and entered a world of fantasy and make believe.

When questioned about the death of Bernice Morden and the human remains found on his farm, Ed Gein told investigators that between 1947 and 1957 he made about forty visits to the local graveyards and exhumed the bodies of recently deceased women that reminded him of his mother. He read the obituaries to see who had just passed away and then he went to the cemetery and took the bodies home where he tanned their skins to make his paraphernalia. All in all, he admitted to robbing nine graves. The police remained suspicious.

How could someone as slight as Ed exhume these bodies and carry them home on his own, and undertake this task in a single night? So while Ed was undergoing interrogation and psychological tests, the police continued to search the land around his farm.

Within the house itself they discovered the remains of ten different women. They could now account for two of those, Bernice Morden and Mary Hogan but what about the other eight? Gein swore that the remaining body parts of eight women were those taken from the local graveyards at Plainfield, Spiritland and Hancock. But the police thought that it was more likely that the remains were from women he had murdered. The only way they could be sure if the remains came from women's corpses was to exhume the graves that Gein claimed he had robbed.

In a small town people talk and when word spread that the police were contemplating digging up the graves local people were both incensed and repulsed. However, the search for the truth outweighed the sensitivities of the locals and the police were finally given permission to dig up a select number of graves to test the veracity of Gein's story. Three test graves were to be exhumed. Sure enough, the three they chose were all empty. They were found exactly as he had described them. The first casket was empty. Gein has been unable to open the second casket because he had lost his pry key. The body was missing from the third grave and Gein had returned rings and some body parts to it. At first, it appeared that Gein had been telling the truth but the police were still digging, literally, and soon there would be another discovery on the farmland that would again raise the issue of whether Gein did in fact murder a third person.

The longer the interrogation went on the more psychologists and police were convinced that Ed Gein was insane and depraved. He had a bizarre reason why he had stolen the bodies. He informed investigators that following the death of his beloved mother he decided he, too, wanted to be a woman so he began to fashion a "woman suit" out of the skins of the bodies so he could pretend to be female. He never enjoyed the company of women so he took great sexual pleasure in peeling the skin from their bodies and wearing it. He wanted to know what it was like to have a vagina and breasts. He also stated that he was fascinated as to how women held so much power over men.

He denied having sex with the bodies simply because they smelled too much. As one investigator was reported as saying: "You couldn't make this shit up." But, how many women did he kill? Initially, he was insistent that he never killed any of the women whose remains were found in the farmhouse with the exception of Bernice Worden. But, after days of intense interrogation he finally admitted that he had in 1954 shot dead a Pine Grove tavern owner, Mary Hogan, and it was her head they found in the paper bag during the search. He couldn't remember any details of the kill because he claimed he was in a "daze" at the time.

During his admissions Gein was completely unemotional and displayed no signs of regret or remorse. He appeared to have no concept of the enormity of the crimes he had committed or the difference between what was right and decent and what was wrong and indecent. But the investigators were not content with just two admissions of murder. There were several other cases where people had died or gone missing in the area in the recent past and he was now the prime suspect.

In fact, in the ten years between 1947 and 1957 Wisconsin police noticed a dramatic increase in the number of people going missing in the area.

On the 1 May 1947 eight year old Georgia Weckler suddenly disappeared on her way home from school. Police aided by several hundred local volunteers searched a ten mile area around Jefferson but to no avail. Her body was never recovered. There were no suspects; the only evidence being tire marks from a Ford car found near where she was last seen. Gein drove a Ford but then so did a lot of people.

In November 1952, two men, Victor "Bunk" Travis and Ray Burgess, stopped for a drink at a bar in Plainfield before heading out to hunt deer. They stayed at the bar for a couple of hours before leaving. Neither of the men nor their vehicle were ever seen again. Despite a massive search the police could find no trace of them. Foul play was suspected.

In 1953 a fifteen year old girl called Evelyn Hartley was babysitting in La Crosse. Her father tried to phone her but when there was no reply he called around to the house. No one answered the door. Looking through a window he noticed one of his daughter's shoes and her spectacles both of which were discarded on the ground. He managed to enter the house through a back basement window. Climbing through the window frame he noticed bloodstains. After searching the house he was convinced that a struggle had taken place. The police were called and discovered more blood stains on the grass outside the house and a bloody hand print on a neighbor's house, Later they found footprints and the girl's second shoe. Despite an extensive search Evelyn could not be found. But several days later they found part of her panties and bra two miles southeast of La Crosse and four miles further, a bloody pair of man's pants was found. Her body was never found. It is thought that Ed Gein was responsible for her death.

All of these people had disappeared in or around Plainfield, Wisconsin but Gein denied any knowledge of them. But then police unearthed human skeletal remains on the farm. They suspected that the body was that of Victor Travis. The remains were taken to a crime lab for examination. But the tests showed that the remains were not male but of a large, middle-aged woman, which Gein claimed was just another graveyard souvenir. Despite their best efforts and due in part to limited resources, the police were unable to implicate Gein in any of the four other cases. The only murders they could pin on him were those of Bernice Worden and Mary Hogan which he eventually gave up after days of intense questioning at Wautoma County Jailhouse. A complication to the investigation arose after Sheriff Art Schley, incensed by Gein and the horror of his depraved actions, assaulted him during questioning by banging his head and face against a brick wall. As a result, lawyers for Gein succeeded in having his initial confession ruled inadmissible. Schley, traumatized by the killings, later died of a heart attack, aged just forty three, before Gein's trial.

Initially, on the 21 November 1957 Ed Gein was arraigned on just one count of first degree murder in Waushara County Court. He pleaded not guilty by reason of insanity. The court found him to be mentally incompetent and, accordingly, unfit for trial.

He was dispatched to the Central State Hospital for the Criminally Insane in Waupan, Wisconsin. (later renamed Dodge Correctional Institution). Afterwards, he was transferred to Mendota State Hospital in Maison, Wisconsin where he was diagnosed with schizophrenia. He underwent a battery of psychological tests, which later concluded that he was indeed emotionally impaired.

Psychologists and psychiatrists who interviewed him asserted that he was not only a schizophrenic but also a "sexual psychopath." Gein's condition was attributed to the unhealthy relationship he enjoyed with his mother as well and his general upbringing. Psychologists asserted that he apparently suffered from conflicting feelings about women, his natural sexual attraction to them and the unnatural attitudes that his mother had instilled in him. This love-hate feeling towards women became exaggerated and eventually developed in to a full-blown psychosis.

Local people were furious that he didn't face the death penalty but the fact is that after Gein spent a period of thirty days in a mental institution and was evaluated as mentally incompetent, he could no longer be tried for first degree murder. Although angry that Gein would not be tried for the death of Bernice Worden there was little the community could do to influence the court's decision.

Sometime after he was sentenced to the mental institution, his farm went up for auction along with some of his personal effects. Thousands of curiosity seekers and rubber-neckers diverged on the small town to see what possessions of Ed Gein's they could buy. Some of the lots to be auctioned off included his car, furniture and musical instruments.

The company that handled the business of selling the lots planned to charge a fee of 50 cents to look at the farmhouse. The citizens of Plainfield were outraged. They believed the Gein's home was quickly becoming a "museum for the morbid" and the town council demanded something be done to put it to an end.

In fact, there were rumors circulating that the new owners would turn the house into a tourist attraction. Although the company was later forbidden to charge an entrance fee to the auction, residents were still not satisfied.

In the early morning of the 20 March, 1958 the Plainfield volunteer fire department was called out to a fire. Ed Gein's farmhouse was ablaze. It quickly burned to the ground, as onlookers watched in silent relief. Police had little doubt that an arsonist was responsible for the blaze because there were no electrical wiring problems with the house. However, after carrying out a thorough investigation, no suspect was ever found. Although the blaze destroyed most of the lots, there were still many things that were salvaged. The main interest was Ed Gein's 1949 maroon Ford sedan which was used to haul dead bodies. After a bidding war it was eventually sold for $760, a sizeable amount of money at the time. The car was bought by an enterprising carnival sideshow operator named Bunny Gibbons. Gibbons called his attraction the "Ed Gein Ghoul Car" and charged carnival-goers 25 cents admission to see it.

After spending ten years in the mental institution where he was recovering, the courts finally decided he was competent to stand trial. The proceedings commenced on the 22 January, 1968, to determine whether Ed Gein was guilty or not guilty by reason of insanity, for the murder of Bernice Worden. The actual trial didn't begin until the 7 November. Gein looked on in a somewhat detached and bemused way as seven witnesses took to the stand. Several of those who testified were lab technicians who performed the autopsy on Mrs. Worden.

The evidence was heavily stacked against the accused and after only one week Judge Robert H. Gollmar reached his verdict. Edward Theodore Gein was found guilty of first-degree murder. However, because he was found to have been insane at the time of the killing, he was later found not guilty by reason of insanity and acquitted. The judge wrote on his court papers that "due to prohibitive costs, Gein was tried for only one murder, that of Mrs. Worden."

Because he was deemed to be legally insane he spent the rest of his life in a mental hospital. The families of Bernice Worden, Mary Hogan and the families of those whose graves were robbed always believed they had been denied justice. They believed Gein escaped the punishment he deserved. Gein remained at a mental institution for the rest of his life where he spent his days happily and in some comfort.

Harold Schechter who wrote the definitive biography of Gein "Deviant: The Shocking True Story of the Original "Psycho" described him as the model patient: "Eddie was happy at the hospital; happier, perhaps, than he'd ever been in his life. He got along well enough with the other patients, though for the most part he kept to himself. He was eating three square meals a day (the newsmen were struck by how much heavier Eddie looked since his arrest five years before). He continued to be an avid reader. He like his regular chats with the staff psychologists and enjoyed the handicraft work he was assigned; stone polishing, rug making, and other forms of occupational therapy. He had even developed an interest in ham radios and had been permitted to use the money he had earned to order an inexpensive receiver. All in all, he was a perfectly amiable, even docile patient, one of the few in the hospital who never required tranquilizing medications to keep his craziness under control. Indeed, apart from certain peculiarities; the disconcerting way he would stare fixedly at nurses or any other female staff members who wandered into his line of vision;— it was hard to tell that he was particularly crazy at all..."

Ed Gein died of respiratory failure on the 26 July 1984 in Stovall Hall at the Mendota Mental Health Institute. He was buried in Plainfield Cemetery next to his mother and adjacent to some of the graves he himself had robbed. His grave was frequently vandalized over the years by souvenir seekers chipping off pieces of his gravestone. The bulk of his gravestone was eventually stolen in 2000. It was later recovered in June 2001 near Seattle. It now lies in storage at the Waushara County Sheriff's Department.

Ed Gein's story has had a lasting effect on Western popular culture as evidenced by its numerous appearances in movies, music and literature. His story was the basis for the plots of several Hollywood blockbusters. He himself inspired the film characters of Norman Bates in *Psycho*, Leatherface in the *Texas Chainsaw Massacre*, and Jame Gumb in *The Silence of the Lambs*. Ed Gein, the original American Psycho, gained notoriety as being one of the most famous of documented cases involving a combination of necrophilia, transvestism and fetishism.

5. RICHARD RAMIREZ (1960-2013)

"I am beyond good and evil. I will be avenged. Lucifer dwells in us all."

- Richard Ramirez

These were the words of Richard Ramirez on the day he was sentenced to death after being convicted for thirteen murders, five attempted murders, eleven rapes and sexual assaults and fourteen burglaries. Ramirez, one of America's most evil and sadistic serial killers was also a serial rapist, a sodomizer, a prolific burglar and a self-avowed Satanist. To the terrified residents of Los Angeles and San Francisco in the summer of 1985 he was known as the *Night Stalker*.

Ramirez was born Richard Leyva Munoz Ramirez in El Paso, Texas on the 29 February 1960. He was the fifth and youngest child of Mexican, Julian Ramirez, and his wife, Mercedes. A former Juarez policeman in Mexico, his father later worked on the railways in Santa Fe. Although hard working and a good family man he was also a strict disciplinarian who suffered from a quick temper which frequently resulted in physical abuse.

While psychologists argue that no child is born evil they recognize that certain factors can help determine their future conduct. Many serial killers including Peter Kurten, George Charles Haigh, Fred West, Raymond Fernandez and others suffered head injuries which altered their personalities in a negative way. Ramirez sustained two serious head injuries as a child. At the age of two, a dresser fell on him resulting in injuries to his forehead which necessitated thirty stitches. Three years later he was knocked unconscious by a park swing. Thereafter, he experienced frequent epileptic seizures. His seizures abated in his early teens but then another factor was to prejudice his wellbeing; the detrimental influence of his older and seriously disturbed cousin, Miguel Ramirez.

The older Ramirez had fought in the Vietnam War and was a decorated Green Beret Veteran. Little did the US Army realize that this decorated soldier had raped, murdered and pillaged his way across Vietnam and had brought home mementos to prove it. He often boasted to his younger cousin of his gruesome exploits and showed him Polaroid photographs he had taken so he could relive the moments. These included photographs of him raping Vietnamese women including some of a rape victim he had just beheaded.

At the age of ten he introduced him to marijuana and taught him his combat skills, and in particular, how to overcome and subdue a victim by stealth alone. Richard or Richie as his family called him, spent many days and nights with his cousin, listening to these lurid stories as he tried to avoid the violent excess of his father's temper.

But there was one incident, in particular, that was a turning point in Richard Ramirez's life. On the 4 May 1973 thirteen year old Richie and his cousin Mike had been hanging out all day drinking beer and getting high when an argument arose between Mike and his wife, Jessie. She complained about him sitting around all day getting high when he should be out finding work. An enraged Mike pulled out a .38 caliber revolver and shot Jessie point blank in the face. The blood spatter covered Richie's face and clothes.

His cousin was tried for the murder. His lawyer argued his combat record in mitigation and pointed out that the atrocities he had both witnessed and personally suffered had seriously damaged his mental stability. He was found not guilty by reason of insanity and sent to the Texas State Mental Hospital in 1977 where he remained for a period of four years. He was then released and continued to be a detrimental influence on his younger cousin.

In that four year period his family noticed a change of personality in the young Richie. He became sullen and withdrawn. He left his parent's home and moved in with his sister Ruth and her husband Roberto. Unfortunately, he was another sexual deviant. Roberto was obsessed with voyeurism and took the young Richie on many nocturnal expeditions. Richie began experimenting with LSD and became involved with Satanism and Devil Worship.

He dropped out of Jefferson High School in the ninth grade and so began a period of acting out his violent sexual fantasies, the seeds of which had been sown by his cousin and continued by his brother in law. He became addicted to violent pornography, in general, and rape and bondage, in particular.

His first serious brush with the law came when he was working in a local Holiday Inn. He would spend his time spying on the guests and using a pass key to rob their valuables. On one occasion he broke into a bedroom and attacked a female guest. After he tied her up he began to rape her when he was interrupted by the returning husband who proceeded to severely beat the culprit. Ramirez was later charged but the case collapsed when the out of state couple refused to testify.

In his late teens or early twenties Ramirez left El Paso and moved to Southern California. He bummed around for a couple of years living like a slacker, smoking weed and eating junk food. His diet was so rich in sugar that his teeth began to rot and he was afflicted with severe halitosis resulting in a seriously bad breath problem. Here he cultivated his love of Satan and became a huge fan of the Australian Rock Band AC/DC.

But it was something darker and more sinister than weed and rock songs that influenced Richie into becoming one of the most reviled and heinous serial killers the world has ever known. An habitual marijuana abuser, Ramirez needed money to feed his habit and he achieved this by simple theft whether it was cars, credit cards, or wallets. But as his addictive habit became greater his crimes became more serious and involved breaking into houses.

There is no evidence that Ramirez was involved in any violent crime in his first few years in Los Angeles. However, he was convicted of some mirror offences for possession and theft. But as the weeks turned into months and the months into years Ramirez realized that he had quite a talent for breaking and entering and it was a very lucrative profession.

As he became more proficient he became bolder and began to linger in the homes he burgled. Soon he was descending into a world of unrelenting violence and depravity. As writer Anthony Bruno so eloquently described it: "Whether by conscious decision or inevitable evolution, Ramirez began to insert himself into his depraved fantasies and actively participate in their re-enactment for his own gratification."

Jennie Vincow was a seventy nine year resident of Glassel Park. On the night of the 28 June 1984 she decided to open the window of her ground floor apartment because it was oppressively hot. Unfortunately, she forgot to close it. Ramirez was stalking the neighborhood and when he noticed the open window; he simply removed the screen and climbed inside.

It wasn't until the following morning that her son, who lived in the same apartment block on one of the upper floors, discovered her body sprawled out on her bed. She had been repeatedly stabbed. Her throat was slashed so deeply that she was almost decapitated. An autopsy later showed that she had been sexually violated. Her apartment had been ransacked and her valuables stolen.

Twenty year old Angela Barrios was driving home to Rosemead, a middle class suburb north east of Los Angeles late on the 17 March 1985. She had just finished her shift and she was tired. She was looking forward to a bite to eat and a long hot shower. As she drove up to the condo she shared with her friend, Dayle Okazaki, she stopped her car in front of the garage and opened the door by way of remote control. Little did she know, as she got out of her car, that a man dressed in black with a navy blue baseball cap pulled down low over his brow, was lurking in the darkness, waiting for her, with a gun in his hand.

As she closed the door the man shot her in the head. She collapsed on the ground. She wasn't dead but she didn't know how seriously injured she was. She thought that if she remained absolutely still and held her breath her attacker might think she was already dead. Her plan worked. Her attacker stepped over her, kicking her body out of the way as he did so and walked into the apartment.

After a while Angela came to and realized her hand was bleeding. Her keys were still in her hand. By sheer luck the bullet had struck the keys and been deflected. Fearing for the safety of her friend she struggled to her feet to sound the alarm. As she staggered out of the garage she heard another gunshot from within.

Disoriented, stunned, frightened and bleeding she began to run but rather than escape to freedom she ran straight into her attacker. She fell over and was certain he was going to shoot her again. But instead he put his gun into his belt and fled. Unfortunately, her thirty four year old roommate, Dayle Okazaki, was not to be so lucky. When Angela staggered into the apartment she found Dayle lying face down on the kitchen floor. The walls, floor, furniture and kitchen appliances were covered in blood spatter. Angela checked to see if she was still breathing but her friend had been shot in the head. She rang 911 and the police arrived in minutes.

But whatever urge Ramirez had that night, it was obvious it had not been satisfied because within an hour he struck again in nearby Monterey Park. His victim this time was a thirty year old Taiwanese native called Tsia-Lian Yu or Victoria to her friends. Her unconscious body was found lying on the ground by an alert policeman checking out a suspicious car. She was still alive, but only just. Her breathing was labored. He called an ambulance but she died in the ambulance before it reached its destination.

The two attacks on the same evening spurred the media into a frenzy. The reports stirred widespread panic and fear among the citizens of Los Angeles. They broadcast a description of the attacker; long curly hair, bulging eyes and wide-spaced rotting teeth. If Ramirez was concerned that the public now had a description of him he didn't show it. He struck again on the 27 March.

Sometime in 1984 Ramirez broke into a house in Whittier, California and stole some valuables. But he made a mental note to return for additional bounty. This time he had a definite *modus operandi* which he planned to use again and again. In the early hours of the 27 March 1985 he broke into the home of sixty four year old Vincent Zazzara. Mr. Zazzara, a former investment counsellor, now owned his own pizzeria. Ramirez expected to find a lot of cash, jewelry and other valuables. At 2:00 a.m. he expected the occupants to be asleep. They were. Ramirez shot Vincent Zazzara in the head with a .22 caliber handgun. The noise woke up his wife, forty four year old attorney, Maxime.

Ramirez proceeded to beat her and tied her up. He demanded to know where the valuables were. While he ransacked their home, Maxime managed to free herself from her restraints. She retrieved a shotgun which was hidden under the bed and tried to shoot her attacker. But the gun was not loaded. An enraged Ramirez shot her three times. He then went to the kitchen, found a large carving knife, returned to the bedroom and in a frenzied attacked stabbed her several times in the neck, face, abdomen, left breast and groin. He gouged out both her eyes. He placed them in a jewelry box and took them with him. The bodies were found the following morning by their son, Peter.

Ramirez had now perfected his *modus operandi* for his crimes. He would choose an apartment in which he would find valuable securities; incapacitate and kill the male and then sexually assault the female before killing her. His motivation had now changed from solely murder for profit to include killing for sexual gratification.

On the 14 May he returned to the Monterey Park area and broke into the home of sixty six year old, Bill Doi, and his fifty six year old disabled wife, Lillian. They were asleep but as Bill Doi woke up and reached for his own personal handgun, Ramirez shot him in the face. He then grabbed him and beat him into unconsciousness. Ramirez entered Lillian's bedroom, battered her with his fists and demanded to know where the valuables were. Once he had subdued her and received the location of the valuables he bound her, ransacked the house and returned to the bedroom and raped Mrs. Doi. He then left. Mr. Doi died that night as a result of his injuries but Mrs. Doi recovered sufficiently to be able to give investigators a description of her attacker.

Two weeks late Ramirez stole a Mercedes and drove to Monrovia where he broke into the home of eighty three year old Mabel Bell and her eighty one year old invalid sister Florence. He bound and bludgeoned Florence with a hammer in her bedroom and then turned his attention to her sister. He bound her, beat her severely with the same hammer and then tried to electrocute her with an electrical cord. After failing in his attempt to rape her, he returned to the invalid Florence and raped the eighty one year old before drawing a pentagram on her thigh with lipstick. He drew further pentagrams in each bedroom. The ladies were only found the following day; both were in a comatose state. Mabel later died from her injuries.

Ramirez's murder spree and rape campaign continued unabated. His next area of choice was Burbank where he entered the home of forty two year old mother of one Carol Kane (sometimes referred to as Ruth Wilson). Carol woke up in her bedroom to find a torchlight shining in her face.

Ramirez placed a gun to her head and demanded to know who else was in the apartment and where she kept her valuables. When she told him she had a twelve year old son he marched her out of her bedroom to her son. He bound the son with handcuffs and locked him in a closet. Ramirez then threw her on the bed, tore off her pink nightgown and proceeded to rape and sodomize her. He then freed her son from the closet and left. The son called 911.

The police now had yet a further description: tall, Hispanic, with long dark hair and foul breath. They were beginning to build a profile. A wave of panic spread like wild fire throughout the city of Los Angeles which was now firmly gripped with fear. The media labelled the killer rapist the *Valley Intruder* and the *Midnight Stalker*. The people put pressure on their politicians who put pressure on the LAPD. The message was clear to the city's police captains; catch this stalker soon or heads will roll. But as the pressure mounted the attacks escalated and by the summer of 1985 he was engaged in a full blown campaign of devastation, rape, murder and destruction.

On the 27 June he raped a six year old girl in Arcadia. The following day the police discovered the body of a thirty two year old woman also in Arcadia. Her throat had been slit. No man, woman or child felt safe. Neighborhoods began setting up vigilante groups to patrol their homes. The police commissioner feared a gradual erosion of law and order. The month of July was a particularly violent month.

Ramirez returned to Arcadia on the night of the 2 July. He arrived at the home of seventy five year old Mary Louise Cannon in a Toyota car he had just stolen. When he found her asleep in her bedroom he picked up a lamp and beat her into a state of unconsciousness. Not content with this, he rummaged through her kitchen drawers until he found a ten inch butcher's knife which he used to repeatedly stab her with and in the process slitting her throat. He ransacked the house for valuables and left. Ramirez was completely indifferent to the age and gender of his victims.

On the 5 July he first attacked sixteen year old Whitney Bennett with a tire iron. She survived but the savage beating necessitated nearly five hundred stiches. Several hours later he drove to Monterey Park where he woke sixty three year old retired nurse, Linda Fortuna, from her sleep. Having robbed the house of all its valuables, he tried unsuccessfully to rape and sodomize her. He then fled. Two days later he returned to Monterey Park and beat sixty one year old Joyce Nelson to death using his fists, his feet and a blunt instrument. He kicked her in the head so violently that he left a shoe print from his runner imbedded in her face.

As Ramirez descended into the darkness of Satanism and Devil worshipping his attacks became more crazed, depraved and violent. On the 20 July he stole a Toyota and purchased a new weapon for his frenzied attacks, a machete. He drove to Glendale and randomly selected the home of sixty eight year old Max Kneiding and his sixty six year old wife, Lela. He burst into their bedroom and hacked them with the machete before shooting them in the head with a .22 caliber handgun. Annoyed that he was unable to locate sufficient valuables he further mutilated their bodies. Max had been butchered so brutally his head was barely attached to his body. There was evidence that Lela had been sexually assaulted. He then drove to Sun Valley for another brutal attack but not before he had fenced the stolen personal effects of Max and Lela Kneiding.

It was shortly after 4:00 a.m. when Ramirez sneaked into the home of the Khovananth family. He began his brutal assault by first shooting the father, Chainarong, in the head as he slept in his bed. Having bound his terrified eight year old son he then beat, raped and sodomized his wife, Somkid before dragging her around the house to locate the family's valuables. During this assault on Somkid he demanded that she swear to Satan that she had surrendered all the couple's money.

But some victims were able to fight back. On the 6 August he broke into the home of the Peterson family in Northbridge. He crept into their bedroom and shot twenty seven year old Virginia in the face. He then shot her husband, thirty eight year old Chris. But Chris, a powerfully built man survived the shot and fought back. Despite having a bullet lodge in his head he managed to chase Ramirez away. Miraculously, both Chris and Virginia survived the attack.

Just two nights after escaping from the Petersons, Ramirez stole a car and drove to Diamond Bar. Here he chose the home of a couple variously described with different names but for our purposes we will refer to them as Mr. EA who was thirty one and his wife Mrs. SA who was twenty seven. He followed his usual *modus operandi* and having broken into their home entered the master bedroom where he found the couple asleep in their double bed. He first killed Mr. EA with a shot to the head and then turned his attention to his terrified wife. He handcuffed and savagely beat her until she revealed the locations of the family's jewelry. He then brutally raped and sodomized her, repeatedly demanding that she swear on Satan that she wouldn't scream during his assaults.

At one point the couple's three year old son, awoken by the commotion, entered the bedroom. Ramirez tied him up and then continued to rape his mother forcing her to perform fellatio on her. When he was finished with her he simply left. Mrs. SA untied her son and sent him to the neighbors for help.

Ramirez decided to switch his attacks to a new territory. The territory he chose was San Francisco.

On the 18 August 1985 police were called to the home of Peter and Barbara Pan in Lake Merced, a suburb of San Francisco. In the master bedroom they found sixty six year old accountant, Peter, and his sixty four year old wife Barbara lying in their blood soaked bed. Peter had been shot at close range in the head with a .22 caliber hand gun. He died instantly. His wife had been savagely beaten, sexually assaulted and also shot in the head but miraculously she was still alive.

An inverted pentagram had been scrawled on the wall in lipstick, together with the words "Jack the Knife." Although Mrs. Pan was to survive the attack she would be an invalid for the rest of her life. A forensic team was employed to scour the home for clues. Doctors removed a bullet from Mr. Pan and recognizing the similarities in this attack and those that had recently taken place in the Los Angeles area they decided to send the bullet to the forensic department of the LAPD to determine if, by any chance, the attacks were linked. Within days the forensic experts reported back. The bullet matched the others recovered from two attacks attributed to the *Night Stalker* in Los Angeles.

They realized that the words "Jack the Knife" were a reference to a song called "The Ripper" by the heavy metal band Judas Priest. Local police determined that the killer had come in through an open window. Slowly but surely they were completing the jigsaw puzzle which would eventually lead to the capture of the *Night Stalker*.

Investigators also concluded that the *modus operandi* of this crime matched another on the 20 February 1985. In that case two elderly women, Mary and Christina Caldwell, had been stabbed to death in their Telegraph Hill apartment. Had the Night Stalker attacked in the Bay area prior to the Pan attack? Was he waging a campaign in both cities? Word had now spread that the *Night Stalker* had move his center of operations from Los Angeles to San Francisco. As the citizens of Los Angeles heaved a huge collective sigh of relief, the citizens of San Francisco, while bolting down the hatches, were demanding instant and meaningful action from the SFPD. It was clear they would not be as patient as their Los Angeles neighbors. As they worked incessantly around the clock to break the case they lucked out.

The manager of a boarding house in the Tenderloin district came forward with some helpful information. He claimed that a man who fit the description of the *Night Stalker* may have stayed at his rooms from time to time over the past eighteen months. He added that the man's teeth were rotten and his breath was awful. When they checked the last room in which he had stayed they discovered a small pentagram drawn in ink on the bathroom door. The guest had checked out on the 17 August. Mr. and Mrs. Pan had been attacked that very night.

Then a fence in the El Sobrante district admitted to recently purchasing some jewelry, including a diamond ring and a set of cufflinks. The items matched those stolen from the Pan household. The police were on a roll. As the authorities inched closer and closer to catching the *Night Stalker*, Ramirez planned a trip out of town. He stole an orange Toyota and drove seventy six miles south of Los Angeles to Mission Viejo. Here he broke into the home of Bill Cairns through a back door. Bill, a twenty nine year old computer programmer and his twenty seven year old fiancée, Carole Smith, had just drifted off to sleep.

On hearing a noise, Bill rubbed the sleep from his eyes and saw an intruder dressed in black pointing a gun to his head. Before he could blink, Ramirez shot him three times. Ramirez then turned his attention to the terrified Carole. He calmly told her that he was the person the media referred to as the *Night Stalker*. He checked the closet and took some neckties with which he bound her ankles and hands. He then began to beat her viciously with his fists while, at the same time, forcing her to swear allegiance to Satan. He demanded to know where the valuables were stashed and after collecting them he returned to the bedroom.

He dragged her by the hair to another room where he raped and sodomized her. He then raped her a second time. Angry that he could find nothing worth stealing he made her swear to Satan that there were no more valuables hidden in the house. Afraid that he would kill her she directed him to a drawer in the bedroom where she knew her boyfriend kept cash. He found the money, counted it and then mocked her, telling her that this was all she was worth. He said that because she had told him where the money was, he would spare her life. But then he turned to her and screamed: "Swear that you love Satan." She replied that she loved Satan.

He made her say it again and again. As she repeated the words he grabbed her by the hair, yanked her to her knees and forced her to perform oral sex on him. When he was satisfied he stepped back and looked at her. She was certain he was now going to kill her. But he didn't. He just laughed and said: "Tell them the Night Stalker was here." He then disappeared out the door.

Carole Smith untied herself and ran to a window to make sure he had left. She just caught him as he got into an old orange Toyota station wagon and drove off. She then called 911 and ran to a neighbor's house for help for her fiancé.

Later surgeons removed two bullets from Bill's head and he survived. Carole's description of the getaway vehicle was corroborated by a neighbor. Thirteen year old James Romero III was in his parent's garage earlier in the night. He was working on his motorcycle when he noticed the old orange station wagon park on the road. He then noticed a "weird looking guy in black" get out of the car. He later saw him leave.

They soon found the stolen car and forensic experts carried out a detailed examination which uncovered a foreign fingerprint on the rear view mirror. They sent the fingerprint to Sacramento for analysis. In a matter of hours a computer search found a match. The print belonged to Ricardo "Richard" Leyva Ramirez. The same print matched a print taken from a window sill at the Pans' house near San Francisco. They didn't yet have the *Night Stalker* but at least they knew who he was. It was only a matter of time before they thought they would catch him, but how much time, and would he kill again in the meantime? Having identified him they released his photograph to the media.

Ramirez took a bus to Tucson, Arizona to visit his brother and was completely unaware that his photograph was being broadcast as the lead story in virtually every major newspaper and television news program across the state of California. When he failed to meet his brother he decided to return to Los Angeles which he did early on the morning of the 31 August. He was still unaware that he was public enemy number one. As he dismounted the bus and strolled through the terminal he walked by a number of policemen who were stalking the area in the hope of capturing him. He walked a few block to a convenience store and then saw his face on the cover of newspapers and magazines. He knew the game was up and fled the store.

But he was soon caught by local people who recognized him and arrested by the police. Following his arrest Ramirez was initially charged with fourteen counts of murder and thirty one other felonies for crimes committed in the Los Angeles area. But there were difficulties in engaging legal counsel to represent him.

He dismissed the first two public defenders who were assigned to represent him. The third found it impossible to act for him. Finally, Daniel Hernandez and Arturo Hernandez, neither of whom had ever defended a potential death penalty case, were appointed. But the two defenders, who were unrelated, persisted and began their representation by filing a number of pre-trial motions. In particular, they sought a change of venue. This was refused but it was the first of many pre-trial motions, all of which had the effect of delaying the actual trial.

While all this was going on in Los Angeles County, the San Francisco authorities were continuing to build their own case against Ramirez. Although they believed he was responsible for four murders, one rape, and ten burglaries their difficulty lay in the fact that they lacked physical evidence. But they had sufficient evidence to proceed with the Peter Pan case and one good case with the resulting conviction would be sufficient to put him away forever.

Meanwhile, back in Los Angeles, it was now three years since he had been arrested and the trial was just about to begin. The number of pre-trial motions lodged by the Hernandez team was nearing the one hundred mark. The case had cost over one million dollars so far and at least one witness had died. It was unprecedented. Jury selection began on the 1 July 1988. The trial judge determined that they would need an additional twelve alternate jurors, all of whom would have to be completely impartial and willing to serve on the jury for up to two years.

Attorney Alan Yochelson joined the prosecution team and because of the frequent absence of Arturo Hernandez the judge appointed another public defender, Ray Clark, to assist the defense. Clark, a humble man, was recognized as a shrewd and worthy attorney.

Halpin opened the case for the prosecution with a two hour long speech stating that the accused was guilty of thirteen murders and thirty felony charges. He would prove this by introducing four hundred exhibits as evidence, including fingerprints, ballistics evidence, and shoe impressions. They could reach no other conclusion but that this man was guilty. Unusually, Hernandez declined to make an opening statement. The prosecution had certain difficulties with their case. It was now four years since the events occurred and some witnesses had problems with memory recall.

Much of the evidence was circumstantial and some of the exhibits were missing. But there was enough evidence there and after one hundred and thirty seven witnesses and five hundred and twenty one exhibits the prosecution rested.

Did the defense have a case? Yes, they had. They claimed that every single one of the eight eyewitnesses were mistaken when they identified Ramirez as the culprit. It wasn't him at all. It was someone else. They claimed that the case against their client was inconclusive and defective. Many of the fingerprints at the crime scenes remained unidentified. Hair and blood samples that were found did not belong to the victims or Ramirez. When the closing statements were made the judge took two days to carefully sum up the issues involved.

After nearly a year, the jury finally started deliberations on the 26 July. Almost two months after they had begun, the jury announced that they had reached a unanimous decision. Ever the coward, Ramirez elected not to attend the verdict hearing.

They found him guilty on each of the forty-three counts. In addition, they affirmed no fewer than nineteen "special circumstances" as to why he should receive the death penalty. When asked by his defense team to attend so they could submit mitigating factors, Ramirez responded that he would not beg for mercy: "Dying doesn't scare me. I'll be in hell. With Satan."

On the 9 November Richard Ramirez was officially sentenced to death. Unfortunately for his victims, Ramirez, one of the most heinous of all serial killers, died of "complications secondary to B-cell lymphoma", in other words, blood cancer, at Marin General Hospital in Greenbrae, California, at 9:10 a.m. on the 7 June 2013 at the age of fifty three, while awaiting execution by the state of California.

His lawyer, Ray Clark, passed away on the 7 January 2014 in Los Angeles. Before his death Clark revealed that the only instructions he ever got from his client was to plead DODDI.

Asked what he meant he replied: "Some other dude did it."

6. FRED WEST (1941-1995)
7. ROSE WEST (1953-

Fred and Rose West were a married couple who became one of Britain's most notorious serial killers. Between 1967 and 1987, Fred alone, and later, with his wife Rosemary, tortured, raped and murdered at least eleven young women and girls, many at the couple's homes. Rose also murdered Fred's stepdaughter, Charmaine, while he was serving a prison sentence for theft. The majority of the murders occurred at their home in 25 Cromwell Street, Gloucester, Gloucestershire, in England. Fred was never found guilty of any of the murders having died before his trial began.

Frederick Walter Stephen West was born on the 29 September 1941 to Walter Stephen West and Daisy Hannah Hill. Fred, the second of six children, was born into a dirt poor family of farm workers in the village of Much Marcle, Herefordshire, in England. Much Marcle is about 120 miles west of London. Fred never bonded with his father and there were rumors, never substantiated, that Fred's mother had taken Fred into her bed from an early age.

Fred was certainly devoted to her. His father was a sexual deviant who enjoyed molesting little girls. He would tell his son that what he did to little girls was completely natural and so he grew up believing that there was absolutely nothing wrong in having sex with little girls and that everyone was at it. Fred left school at fifteen having learned nothing and reached a level of education common for a seven year old. Fred's first paid job was as a farm laborer.

Even at an early age Fred was obsessed with girls and sex and motor bikes. On the 28 November 1958 Fred had an accident on the bike and suffered serious head injuries. He remained unconscious for several days and suffered extensive injuries including a steel plate inserted into his head to keep his shattered skull together. He had numerous broken bones and fractures including a severely broken nose. His family claim that Fred was never the same after that accident. Several months after the accident, Fred met the first love of his life, Catherine Bernadette Costello, or Rena to her friends.

Unlike the other girls in the village Rena was an experienced sixteen year old woman who wasn't a virgin. Fred's crude ways didn't turn her off and neither did the constant demands for sex. Rena fell hopelessly in love with Fred but by September 1960, struggling to find work and with money constantly in short supply Rena decided to move back to Scotland and left Fred behind in Much Marcle. Shortly afterwards, Fred was out for an evening at Ledbury Youth Club when he fell off a fire escape and landed on his head. He was taken by ambulance to the cottage hospital in Ledbury.

This was his second period of unconsciousness but unlike the first he came round after twenty four hours. However, it is clear that as a result of the fall he suffered permanent, albeit, mild brain damage causing a change in his personality, which was not for the better. He became quickly irritable and short tempered.

In September 1962, Fred met up again with his first love Catherine "Rena" Costello. Rena was now working as a prostitute and was already pregnant by another man. In spite of this, Fred and Rena married on the 17 November 1962 and moved to Coatbridge, Lanarkshire. Three months later, on the 22 February Rena gave birth to a baby daughter, Charmaine Carol. Charmaine's biological father was from Pakistan. Everyone knew Rena was pregnant but assumed the child she was carrying belonged to Fred.

Fred and Rena then claimed that their child had died at birth and that they adopted Charmaine. In July 1964, Rena and Fred had their own child, a daughter they named Anna Marie. During that time, Rena and Fred met Anna McFall, whose boyfriend had been killed in an accident.

Eventually, Rena left Fred in 1966 due to his incessant sex demands and returned to Scotland with Isla McNeill while Anna McFall, who had become infatuated with Fred, remained with him and the two children. Rena continued to visit her children every few months. In August 1967 Anna McFall, who was eight months pregnant with Fred's child, simply vanished. She was never reported missing and her remains were found in June 1994.

In September 1967, Rena returned to live with Fred but only remained for a year. She left all the children in Fred's care. But by this stage, Fred had fallen for another woman who was soon to become his soul mate and the love of his life. Her name was Rose Letts and she was just fifteen.

Rosemarie Pauline Letts was born on the 29 November 1953 in Barnstaple, Devon, England to William Andrew Letts and Daisy Gwendoline Fuller after a difficult pregnancy. She was one of three daughters. Her father who was in the army was a strict disciplinarian who was known to bully his wife and beat her and the children. Both her parents suffered from mental problems.

When baby Rose was brought home from Highfield Maternity Home in Northam it was immediately clear that she was unlike her other siblings. She developed a habit of violently rocking herself in her cot. When she was put in a pram, even with the brake on, she would rock so hard that the pram would move across the room. As she grew older the rocking was confined to her head and the rocking would continue for hours on end until she almost entered a semi-comatose state. Despite this worrying sign her parents never deemed it necessary for her to receive any medical attention for this condition.

Rose performed poorly in school. She was pretty much hopeless at everything and her classmates called her "Dozy Rosie". Her laziness was not confined to school. At home, she refused to carry out her share of the chores. The family moved around a bit and eventually settled in the village of Bishop's Cleve, five miles from Cheltenham in Gloucestershire. It was also just three odd miles from Much Marcle where Fred was from.

Fred first met Rose on her fifteenth birthday on the 29 November 1968. He was still married to Rena Costello at the time and was twenty seven. He told her that his wife had deserted him and left him with two children to look after. Rose always loved children and she was now hooked. She moved into the caravan with Fred who was now developing an unhealthy and perverse interest in kinky sexual practices. Having introduced her into deviant sex Fred now wanted to see her having sex with other men.

He persuaded her to become a prostitute. Unfortunately, the children didn't particularly get on with Rose. Germaine, in particular, did not take too kindly to being told what to do by someone less intelligent than her and only ten years older. She contacted her mum Rena Costello who travelled down to see them. This was the first time Rena met Rose. Rose persuaded Fred that for them to have any chance of surviving as a family they would need to move to a proper house and several months later, in June1974, they moved to 25 Midland Road in Gloucester.

On the 17 October 1970 Rose gave birth to her first child, Heather Ann. But then disaster struck. Fred's thieving had got out of hand and he was sent to prison for ten months.

Rose found it very difficult to cope and began taking out her frustrations on the children. Rose brought the children to see Fred in prison several times, the last visit being on the 15 June.

At that visit Fred told Rose that there was a possibility he might get parole in a matter of days. Between that visit and his release a few days later Rose murdered Charmaine at 25 Midland Road. On his release, Fred simply accepted it.

Fred knew it would only be a matter of time before Rena would come looking for her daughter Charmaine. When Rena discovered that her daughter was no longer living with Fred and Rose she went to see him. Fred then decided to kill Rena to keep her quiet and then mutilated her body before burying her in the countryside.

On the 29 January 1972 Fred married Rose at the Gloucester Register Office. Later they bought 25 Cromwell Road to help develop Rose's ever growing prostitution business. Fred also built a torture chamber in the basement. There were rumors at the time that Fred was now part of a satanic cult and involved in procuring victims for their sacrificial rituals. They also abducted and tortured young girls for their own sexual gratification. Those victims included Caroline Owen and Lynda Gough. Lynda died during one of these torture sessions. They buried her in the garden.

Their next victim was fifteen year old Caz Cooper. They abducted Caz on the 10 November 1973. They brought her home and sexually tortured her for hours before finally killing her and burying her remains in the garden.

Lucy Partington did not fit the usual victim profile for Fred and Rose West. Aged twenty one, Lucy was a final year student at Exeter University. They abducted her from a bus stop and tortured her for several days before she died from her injuries. Her disappearance caused a huge nationwide manhunt but no one thought that Fred the Shred or Dozy Rosie were involved.

In fact, life was good for the West family which now consisted of Fred, Rose, their sons Stephen (born August 1973), and Steven (Fred's illegitimate child), and Fred's daughter Anna Marie. No one knew that beyond this façade of happy families the Wests were abducting and torturing young girls in the basement of their home at 25 Cromwell Road.

Therese Siegenthaler was a twenty one year old woman from Switzerland who was studying Sociology in college. The Wests picked her up when she was hitchhiking and brought her home to their torture chamber. They bound her arms and legs using a rope and then raped her several times. When they had killed her Fred set about chopping up her body.

Fred had a habit of first decapitating his victims because, in his own words, he wanted to make sure they were dead before he cut them up. Therese's body was buried in a sump-like hole in the cellar over which Fred later built a false chimney breast. Seven months later, fifteen year old Shirley Hubbard was to join the other bodies buried under 25 Cromwell Road.

Juanita was an eighteen year old attractive girl with brown hair and of medium height. She had been one of the West's lodgers a few years earlier. They picked her up while out walking and brought her to the torture chamber where, like the others, they suspended her from the ceiling and eventually killed her. When they didn't bring victims home Fred and Rose would rape their own child Anne-Marie. The abuse was constant.

Rose met Shirley Robinson when she was eighteen and working in the Gloucester area as a prostitute. Rose persuaded her to come back to 25 Cromwell Road and use that as a base. Shirley liked both men and women and this excited Fred and Rose. Soon a *ménage-a-trois* had developed between the three. Fred did not seem displeased when Rose was made pregnant by one of her "colored punters", in fact, he seemed quite pleased, adding that blacks made better breeders.

Rose didn't seem that put out either when Shirley announced that she was pregnant with Fred's child. But as Shirley's pregnancy developed Rose's personality became increasingly eccentric. After a while Rose decided that Shirley was getting too close to Fred. Her body was hacked to shreds. Meanwhile, Fred and Rose's relationship returned to "normal" and Rose gave birth to another child, a baby daughter called Louise, on the 17 November 1978.

Ally Chambers was a teenager Fred and Rose groomed for sexual abuse. She used to visit them at Cromwell Road. It wasn't long before they tortured, raped, murdered and decapitated her.

When Anna Marie moved out of Cromwell Road, Fred and Rose began to torture and rape their other child Heather. Eventually Heather broke down and confessed to a friend, Denise, what really was going on in her house. She was determined to escape. But before she did Fred and Rose killed her and buried her in the garden. They told everyone she had secured a job in Devon. Amazingly no one in Social Services ever investigated any of these claims. The Wests thought they would never be caught. They were wrong.

Detective Constable Hazel Savage was asked to investigate a complaint against the Wests. Right from the get go she knew something was seriously wrong. Children had gone missing and she couldn't find any trace of them. She was convinced that Fred and Rose West were responsible for their deaths. She tried to obtain a warrant to search their garden and at first it was refused but she didn't give up. She continued her enquiries until eventually her superiors agreed.

On Thursday morning the 6 August 1992 the police arrived at 25 Cromwell Road to investigate allegations of child abuse and they brought with them a search warrant. Rose was arrested for aiding and abetting the rape of a thirteen year old girl and for obstructing the police. Fred was arrested and taken to the station where he was questioned about possession of pornography, rape and buggery.

Anna Marie gave DC Savage a detailed statement about her treatment at the hands of her parents but despite extensive searches she could not find her older sister, Heather, who would have been a key witness in corroborating the charges. Not only could she not trace Heather, she couldn't track down Rena, Fred's first wife or Charmaine, Rena's daughter.

Rose was allowed to return home but Fred was remanded in custody. The remaining children were placed in care. Although they both underwent extensive questioning concerning the abuse allegations they were also asked about the disappearance of Heather. Neither cracked under this pressure but their answers were flippant, evasive and contradictory. The trial was fixed for the 6 June 1993.

In the dock Fred West pleaded not guilty to three charges of rape, one charge of buggery and one charge of cruelty. Rose West was charged with encouraging him to have sex with a child and with cruelty. She also pleaded not guilty.

The case collapsed that morning when the prosecutor informed the judge that the complainant and a second essential witness were refusing to give evidence. Fred and Rose were off the hook, yet again.

The case against them may have collapsed but DC Savage was determined to find out what had happened to the three family members who had apparently vanished, Rena, Germaine and Heather.

She had a hunch and that hunch would not go away. It is a measure of the high esteem in which she was held that when she went back again to her superiors in February 1994 that they relented and agreed she could apply for a warrant to search the house and gardens. A Section Eight search warrant was granted on the 23 February 1994.

At 1:25 p.m. the following morning, the police arrived at 25 Cromwell Road to execute the warrant and began digging the following day. They brought Fred in for questioning and he immediately admitted he had killed his daughter Heather West and that they were searching in the wrong part of the garden. But they didn't stop digging and soon more and more bodies were discovered. They were both charged with multiple murders.

On the 30 June at Gloucester Magistrates Court, Fred and Rose West were each charged with nine murders and remanded in custody. On the morning of the 1 January 1995 Fred wrote a note to Rose: "To Rose West, Happy new year darling. All my love, Fred West. All my love for ever and ever." At 11:30 a.m. Fred collected his lunch and was locked into his cell. He then, apparently, took his own life.

The trial of Rose West of ten counts of murder and two of rape and indecent assault was fixed for the 3 October

1995. West pleaded not guilty to all charges. The evidence against her was purely speculation. Her husband, Fred West, had already admitted to the murders. He also claimed that she had absolutely nothing to do with the killings.

Her defense was run by Richard Ferguson QC an experienced criminal lawyer but their case was plagued by mistakes. When Rose West decided to give evidence the jury took an instant dislike to her. When the trial ended the jury deliberated for two days. They had reached a verdict in relation to counts one and ten. They found Rose West guilty of the murder of Germaine West and Heather West.

They were sent back to deliberate on the other eight counts. Less than two hours later they found Rose West guilty of the murder of Shirley Robinson. The jury were then sent home. Just before one o'clock the following day the jury reached a verdict in relation to all the seven counts of murder, Guilty on all counts.

Mr. Justice Mantell's sentence was brief: "Stand up. Rosemary Pauline West, on each of the ten counts of murder of which you have been unanimously convicted by the jury, the sentence is one of life imprisonment. If attention is paid to what I think, you will never be released. Take her down."

Certain key questions raised during the investigations remain unanswered. The first is if Fred West and Rose West were assisted by a third party in the killings. Did Fred West really cut up all those bodies on his own? What about all the blood? There was no evidence of the cellar floor being soaked in blood. How was the blood disposed of? Were the bodies hacked in the cellar of number 25 Cromwell Street or were they brought somewhere else. On several occasions West admitted that he did not act alone, that he was protecting someone, and it wasn't Rose West as many people think.

There are suggestions that he was protecting a senior figure in a Satanic cult in Gloucestershire. However, these suggestions have yet to be proved. Finger and toe bones hold a particular significance in relation to satanic rituals. Why did Fred West remove these bones? Where are they? Three times West was asked by police why the bones were not buried with the rest of the bodies. Three times he said he had no comment to make on the matter.

Gordon Burns is the author of a book, well worth reading, called Happy Like Murderers (1998) about the West killings. In December 1998 he was interviewed for over an hour by the Chief Constable of Gloucestershire police, Tony Butler, and DCI Terry Moore, regarding his theories on the whereabouts of numerous bones which were missing from several of West's victims. Referring to the bones, Moore said that there are various theories but nothing has come to light. The secret has gone to the grave with Fred. And Rose is not saying anything.

Burns suggests that Fred West may have buried the bones near Pittville Park in Cheltenham, as the park is close to the bus stop where Fred and Rose first met in 1970. He believes the location holds an almost spiritual significance for the Wests. Is this where Fred West went the day the police arrived to dig up his back garden or did he visit his prominent and significant mystery accomplice?

From investigations I have carried out it seems certain that Fred West and his brother John worked for a witches coven in Gloucestershire and that many of the victims were murdered "to order" and used as devil sacrifices. Bones were removed and buried separately which is common in witchcraft. It's unlikely the Wests were members of the coven because of their lower class origins. It is usual for coven members to be rich professionals. In fact, some of the murders are likely to have been committed by members of the coven as Fred West, when questioned, could only provide vague recollections and no details of many of the deaths. Even when caught, he was terrified of the people he was protecting. But they couldn't trust him to remain silent.

The question as to whether Fred West really did commit suicide in his cell has never been satisfactorily answered. Why would he want to commit suicide? He told his significant adult Janet Leach that he had plans for when he got out of prison. She believes he was too much of a coward to kill himself. He told her that he was part of a group of sexual deviants called the cult who used a farm to torture and kill their victims and that he had to protect their identities. If he didn't, his life was in danger.

Furthermore, on the 29 April 1994 rather than speak to his interview team, which would be recorded, he handed them a note. It read: "I have not and still cannot tell you the whole truth…from the very first day of this enquiry my main concern has been to protect another person or persons."

It is unlikely Fred West committed suicide. It's more than likely he was murdered to prevent him telling the truth in court. And if you consider that far-fetched then ask yourself about the circumstances surrounding the death of his brother John. John was part of this cult which assisted him in some of the murders and was in custody on multiple rape charges. He too died, and again the official story was that he committed suicide by hanging himself in his garage on the 28 November 1996 while awaiting a verdict in a multiple rape case.

Were Fred and his brother John murdered by members of the Witches Coven to ensure that they did not reveal their identities? There are many commentators who believe they were murdered and that the leader of the Coven was an influential officer in the Gloucestershire Police Force.

8. JEFFREY DAHMER (1960-1984)

"The only motive that there ever was was to completely control a person--a person I found physically attractive. And keep them with me as long as possible, even if it meant just keeping a part of them."

– Jeffrey Dahmer

Jeffrey Dahmer was one of America's most notorious serial sex killers. He was born on the 21 May, 1960 in West Allis, Wisconsin, to Joyce Annette (née Flint) and Lionel Herbert Dahmer. He was their first born. Dahmer's father Lionel, who was of German extraction, was a Chemistry student at Marquette University. His mother Joyce, who was of Welsh extraction, was employed as a teletype machine instructor. Initially, it was a loving household with both parents doting on him and as a toddler Jeffrey wanted for nothing.

Jeffrey was a happy child until he reached the age of six. He then appeared to undergo a personality change following a minor surgical operation to correct a double hernia. Or, perhaps it was because of the birth of his brother or a combination of both but, for whatever reason, he suddenly became increasingly insular and lacking in self-esteem. Psychologists have suggested that when his brother was born much of his parent's attention became focused on the younger boy which increased Jeffrey's sense of neglect. He himself described his early years as a time of "extreme tension" with his parents constantly arguing.

By the time he was eight the family had moved home eight times. It was known that his mother Joyce was often tense and argumentative not just with her husband but also with neighbors. She also required a lot of attention from her husband who spent less and less time at home. Desperately unhappy and in an effort to seek attention his mother once attempted suicide from an overdose of Equanil pills to which she was addicted.

At school, teachers remember Jeffrey as a shy and timid boy who appeared to be neglected by his parents. Despite this he made friends and was initially fascinated by insects and then animals. But it was not a particularly healthy preoccupation. Jeffrey was more interested in dead animals than living ones and would often collect roadside kills, dismember them and store the parts in glass jars. He would then try to re-assemble the parts to see how they "fitted together." This unhealthy interest turned into an obsession and he was once reprimanded for impaling a dog's head on a stake behind his house.

In October 1966, while Joyce was pregnant with her second child, the family moved to Doylestown. His brother David was born on the 18 December. During this time his father, Lionel, graduated and secured employment as an analytical chemist in Akron.

The family only stayed in Doylestown for two years before moving to Bath, Ohio. His father noticed that Jeffrey was becoming disengaged, uptight and lacked friends.

He was enrolled in Revere High School and right from the get go was considered odd and, accordingly, he was largely ignored by his fellow students. Even at this age he was regarded as a substance abuser, constantly smuggling beer and spirits into school and hiding them in his locker. Although not hugely popular with his peers, his teachers regarded him as polite and highly intelligent although somewhat apathetic. He wasn't a complete loner at school. He enjoyed tennis and was, for a short period, a member of the school band.

It was around this time that he began experimenting with his sexuality. But it wouldn't be until 1991 that he fully accepted that he was homosexual. He later admitted that initially he was more pre-occupied with fantasies of seeking dominance and control over subservient partners rather than with actual sex.

These fantasies grew to involve dissection in one form or another. At the age of sixteen, he planned to ambush and attack a particular male jogger he fancied, render him unconscious and perform sexual acts on him.

This was no idle fantasy and one day he hid in the bushes with a baseball bat waiting for his prey. Fortunately for the jogger, he decided to change his route that particular day and Dahmer gave up on the plan.

Dahmer was known as something of a prankster at High School and often engaged in these pranks to amuse his classmates and to attract attention. Or perhaps, they were a way in which he thought he might make himself more popular. These pranks included bleating, pretending to suffer an epileptic fit, making fun of invalids, and knocking over items both at school and at local stores. They became so talked about that they were referred to as "doing a Dahmer."

Dahmer enjoyed the fact they brought him notoriety and a certain cult status. By the time he was seventeen his academic career was suffering and his grades plummeted. It wasn't that he couldn't keep up. It was more a case that he just didn't care. His social life was no better and he became increasingly more introverted and isolated.

A private tutor hired by his parents had limited success. This downward trend may have had something to do with the difficulties his parents were experiencing. They were attending counselling sessions to try and resolve personal differences and avoid separating. The counselling sessions failed to resolve their issues and his parents decided to divorce. Initially, they remained amicable but as tensions grew, both parents began to frequently quarrel in the presence of their sons.

In early 1978, Lionel Dahmer decided to leave the family home and moved into a nearby motel. The separation had a detrimental effect on Jeffrey and he began to drink heavily. Most of the arguments between his parents centered on custody of his younger brother David.

When his mother was awarded custody, and since Jeffrey had reached eighteen, she decided to leave Jeffrey in the family residence and moved in with family members of her own in Chippewa Falls in Wisconsin. Jeffrey was left in the house without food or money. Needless to say, he felt completely abandoned.

Shortly afterwards on the 18 June Jeffrey picked up an eighteen year old hitchhiker called Steven Mark Hicks who was on his way to a rock concert in Lockwood Corners and persuaded him to come home with him for a couple of beers. They spent the next few hours drinking and listening to music. They then had sex. But when Steven insisted on leaving an argument ensued. Jeffrey left the room and returned with a 10lb dumbbell and struck him twice from behind as he sat in a chair. The blows didn't kill him. They merely rendered him unconscious so Jeffrey proceeded to strangle the boy with the bar of the dumbbell.

He then stripped him naked and masturbated over his dead body. The following morning he dragged the body under the crawl space of his house where he dissected it.

He later put the body parts in plastic bags and buried them in a shallow grave in the woods behind his house. Several weeks later he dug up the remains and pared the flesh from the bones. He then dissolved the flesh in acid before flushing the entire solution down the toilet. He crushed the bones with a sledgehammer. It was his first kill and it felt good.

Six weeks afterwards, Lionel Dahmer, accompanied by his new fiancé, returned to live in the house. Jeffrey enrolled at Ohio State University to study business. Due to the fact that he began drinking excessively he was forced to abandon his University career after a single term.

When his father became aware of his son's alcohol addiction he persuaded him to join the army and, somewhat surprisingly he agreed. He enlisted in the U.S. Army in January 1979 and trained as a medical specialist at Fort Sam Houston. In July 1979 he was posted to Baumholder in West Germany where he served as a combat medic. Military reports suggest that Dahmer was "an average or slightly above average" soldier.

He was repeatedly reprimanded for disobeying orders, failing to report for duty and reporting for duty while intoxicated. In fact, at one stage in February 1981, the army placed him in a drug rehabilitation program.

When this didn't help solve the problem he was considered unsuitable for military service and was honorably discharged. The army gave him a free airline ticket to anywhere in America he wanted to go to and fed up with the cold weather in Germany he opted for Miami Beach, Florida.

Here, he worked in a coffee shop and lived in a motel. However, due to excessive drinking, he never had enough money to pay his rent and was eventually evicted. He continued to work in the coffee shop and sleep on the beach until September 1981 when he called his father and asked him if he would send him enough money to return home to Ohio. His father duly obliged.

Jeffrey returned to Ohio and briefly stayed with his father and new step mother but his drinking continued unabated. He was only twenty one but was already a chronic alcoholic. After just two weeks he was arrested for drunk and disorderly conduct, fined sixty dollars and given a suspended ten-day jail sentence. A few months later, he went to live with his grandmother in West Allis. He tried hard to please her by accompanying her to church, undertaking chores around the house and actively looking for employment. Despite the fact that he was secretly drinking he managed to find employment as a phlebotomist at the Milwaukee Blood Plasma Center. Unfortunately, he was made redundant after ten months. For the next two years he remained unemployed surviving on pocket money from his grandmother.

It is believed that a possible factor in his redundancy was the fact that he was arrested for indecent exposure at Wisconsin State Fair Park, where he exposed himself to a crowd of women and children earning him a fifty dollar fine.

1985 proved to be an eventful year for Jeffrey Dahmer. In January he secured employment as a mixer at the Milwaukee Ambrosia Chocolate Factory. But the following month an incident occurred which rekindled the homosexual tendencies he thought he had suppressed. One day, while reading in the West Allis Public Library, he was propositioned by a stranger who offered to perform fellatio on him. Although he ignored the advance the incident stirred in his mind the fantasies of control and dominance he had developed as a teenager. He now began to check out the Milwaukee gay scene and frequent its gay bars, bookstores and bathhouses. By the end of the year he was a frequent bathhouse visitor. He enjoyed several sexual encounters but they became increasingly abnormal.

Any movement by his sexual partner during the sex act annoyed him intensely. He later stated: "I trained myself to view people as objects of pleasure instead of people." In order to achieve his desired objective he began the practice of administering sleeping pills to his partners, sometimes lacing their drinks with sedatives. Shortly after this, his bathhouse membership was revoked and he then began using hotel rooms.

In March 1987, following another incident of indecent exposure he was sentenced to one year's probation and ordered to undergo counseling.

In November 1987, nine years after his first murder, Dahmer was to kill again. While cruising the gay bars he met a twenty five year old Ontonagon native called Steven Tuomi. After sharing a few drinks together he persuaded him to accompany him to the Ambassador Hotel where he rented a room for the night. His plan was to render him unconscious and then have sex with him.

The following morning he awoke to find himself in bed with Tuomi lying beneath him. Tuomi's chest had been crushed and blood was trickling from his mouth. Dahmer claimed to have no recollection of what transpired that night. He later told investigators that he "could not believe this had happened."

He put the body in a newly purchased suitcase, and brought it back to his grandmother's house where he dismembered it. He filleted the bones from the body before cutting the flesh into pieces small enough to handle. The flesh was placed inside plastic garbage bags and the bones crushed with a sledgehammer. The remains were, with the exception of the head, then dumped in the trash. He retained the head and used it as a stimulus for masturbation.

Although he claims he can't remember how his second victim died, Dahmer was certainly acquiring a taste for killing. Two months later he met a fourteen year-old Native American male prostitute called James Doxtator. Dahmer brought him back to his room at his grandmother's house. Here he was drugged, raped and then strangled. He left the boy's body in the cellar for a week before disposing of it in the same way he did with Tuomi.

On the 24 March, 1988, Dahmer picked up a twenty two year old bisexual called named Richard Guerrero outside a gay bar called The Phoenix and offered him $50 to simply spend the night with him. Richard was drugged and then strangled with a leather strap. Then Dahmer performed oral sex upon the corpse. His body was dismembered and his remains again disposed of in the trash. Dahmer retained his head for subsequent sexual gratification.

When Dahmer's grandmother complained to him about his habit of bringing young men back to the house he decided to move to a one-bedroom apartment on North Twenty-fifth Street. Immediately afterwards he was once again arrested. This time it was for the most serious offense yet; drugging and sexually fondling a thirteen year old boy whom he had lured to his home on the pretext of posing nude for photographs.

He was convicted in January 1989 of second-degree sexual assault and of enticing a child for immoral purposes.

Sentencing was put back until May, 1989. Before sentence was imposed Dahmer registered his fifth kill, a twenty four year old aspiring model called Anthony Sears. Because he found his victim "exceptionally attractive" he preserved both his head and genitalia in acetone.

Dahmer was sentenced on the 23 May 1989. He spoke eloquently in his defense and claimed that he was very sorry and had seen the error of his ways. He received five years' probation and one year in the House of Correction, with daily work release. He was also registered as a sex offender.

On his release he moved into Apartment 213, 924 North 25th Street bringing the head and genitals of Anthony Sears with him. Within a week he had killed his sixth victim, Raymond Smith. Afterwards he spray painted his skull and placed it alongside that of Anthony Sears.

The following month he murdered Edward Smith. Three months later he murdered Ernest Miller by severing his carotid artery. Dahmer wrapped Miller's heart, biceps and portions of flesh from the legs in plastic bags and placed them in the fridge for later consumption. He had now added cannibalism to his list of gruesome crimes.

His next victim was twenty two year old father of one David Thomas. It was five months before he killed again; Curtis Straughter and then Errol Lindsey. By 1991, fellow residents of the Oxford Apartments were complaining of the smells emanating from Apartment 213 but Dahmer told the manager they came from tropical fish that had recently died.

Dahmer's behavior was becoming increasingly more bizarre. On the 26 May he was walking on Wisconsin Avenue when he met a fourteen year old boy called

Konerak Sinthasomphone. He persuaded the somewhat reluctant boy to return to his apartment to pose for some Polaroid photographs. Here he was drugged into unconsciousness and fellated.

But this time Dahmer decided to experiment on his victim and drilled a single hole into his skull. He then injected muriatic acid into his frontal lobe. He wanted to see the effect it might have on him. He later claimed that the reason he did this was because he thought the boy had seen the body of Tony Hughes in the apartment. Dahmer had killed Hughes three days earlier. As the boy lay unconscious Dahmer had a few beers before leaving to visit a nearby bar.

When he returned several hours later Dahmer discovered the boy sitting naked on the corner of 25th and State. He was talking in Laotian and surrounded by three hysterical women. Dahmer told the women who included his neighbor Sandra Smith and her daughter, that the boy was his lover and that they had a lover's tiff and then proceeded to lead him to his apartment by the arm. The women objected and informed him that they had already phoned 911.

When Officers John Balcerzak and Joseph Gabrish arrived on the scene Dahmer calmly told them that Sinthasomphone was his nineteen year old boyfriend, that they had had a lover's tiff and because of that the boy had drunk too much. He told them that he often acted like this after drinking too much.

The police believed the story but the women, exasperated, began arguing with the police telling them that the boy was bleeding from his rectum and had earlier refused to go back into the apartment with Dahmer. Despite their protestations, during which they were told to "butt out," "shut the hell up" and stop interfering the police officers simply put a towel around the boy and led him back to the apartment to verify the accuracy of what they had been told. Back in the apartment Dahmer showed the officers the two semi-nude Polaroid pictures he had taken earlier. Despite the foul smell of the decomposing body of Hughes the officers accepted Dahmer's version of events and left telling Dahmer to take care of his young friend. Had the officers run a simple background check on Dahmer they would have seen he was a convicted child molester under probation. It was the closest he had come yet to getting caught. When they left Dahmer killed the boy with a further injection of muriatic acid into his brain.

Dahmer's urges were now way out of control and he believed he could kill with immunity. By the summer of 1991 he was killing nearly one young man every week. The *modus operandi* was always the same; he would lure them back to the apartment, drug them, have sex with them, kill them, have sex again with the corpse, dismember their bodies, sometimes eat their flesh and retain their skulls before disposing of the remains.

Matt Turner (20), Jeremiah Weinberger (23), Oliver Lacy (23) and Joseph Bradehoft (25) were soon added to the list of victims. Like many serial killers, they become empowered with each kill and arrive at a state where they believe they will never get caught. It is at this stage that they begin to get sloppy. It was only a matter of time before the same would happen to Dahmer and his time had now arrived.

On the 22 July 1991, Dahmer enticed thirty two year old Tracy Edwards back to his apartment where he tried to handcuff him before brandishing a knife and threatening him. At one point he placed his head on Edward's chest, listened to his heartbeat and informed him he intended to cut out his heart and eat it. It wasn't a joke.

Eventually, Edwards managed to calm him down before a scuffle broke out and he was able to escape. He managed to flag down two police officers, Rolf Mueller and Robert Rauth, and explained to them that a "weird dude" had handcuffed him and tried to kill him with a large knife. He persuaded them to come back with him to the apartment.

When they arrived Dahmer opened the door and invited the three of them inside. He admitted to handcuffing Edwards but gave no reason. Edwards told Officer Rolf Mueller that the key to the handcuffs was in a bedside dresser in the bedroom. Mueller entered the bedroom and found the knife under the bed. When he opened the bedside locker he saw a large number of Polaroid photographs. As he examined the photographs which he noticed had been taken in that very apartment he realized that they were pictures of human bodies in various stages of dismemberment. He then showed them to his colleague saying: "These are for real."

On seeing this, Dahmer attempted to escape but was overpowered. The officers called for back-up and continued to search the apartment. When Officer Mueller opened the refrigerator he discovered the freshly severed head of a black male placed on the bottom shelf. Later, the Criminal Investigation Bureau carried out a forensic search and uncovered a total of four severed heads in the kitchen and a further seven skulls in the bedroom and closet.

The refrigerator also contained two human hearts and arm muscle, each wrapped inside plastic bags. The freezer contained an entire torso, plus a bag of human organs and flesh stuck to the ice at the bottom. Other human remains discovered included two entire skeletons, a pair of severed hands, two severed and preserved penises, a mummified scalp and in a 57-gallon drum, three further dismembered torsos dissolving in an acid solution. The chief medical officer was later to comment: "It was more like dismantling someone's museum than an actual crime scene."

Detectives Patrick Kennedy and Patrick Murphy spent in excess of sixty hours interrogating Dahmer over the finds. Throughout these interrogations Dahmer waived his right to an attorney and stated he wanted to make a complete confession. In the course of that confession he stated that: "I had created this horror and it only makes sense I do everything to put an end to it."

He confessed to sixteen murders he had committed in Wisconsin, giving details of the circumstances surrounding each one. He also mentioned a further victim, Steven Hicks, that he had killed in Ohio. He informed them that he had committed necrophilia with several of his victims' bodies and had performed sexual acts with their viscera while dismembering their bodies.

He also confessed to cannibalism and said he had consumed hearts, livers, biceps and portions of thighs. He explained that he had been completely swept along with a compulsion to kill, adding: "It was an incessant and never-ending desire to be with someone at whatever cost. Someone good looking, really nice looking. It just filled my thoughts all day long."

When asked about the preservation of the skulls and skeletons he stated that he had intended to build a private shrine consisting of an altar adorned by the skulls, with the two skeletons side by side illuminated by blue globe lighting in front of which he intended to worship in a black leather chair.
The altar was to be dedicated to himself to meditate: "It

was a place where I could feel at home." The more he confessed the more they realized he was insane.

On the 25 July 1991 he was charged with four counts of murder and on the 22 August this was increased to fifteen murders in Wisconsin. Later, he was charged with the murder of Steven Hicks in Ohio. On the 13 January 1992 he pleaded guilty but insane to fifteen counts of murder. His trial began on the 30 January in Milwaukee. The only relevant issue was whether he suffered from either a mental or a personality disorder.

The defense provided three expert witnesses; the prosecution three and the court invited two independent expert witnesses. The defense experts argued that Dahmer was insane due to his necrophilic drive. Dr. Fred Berlin testified that the accused was incapable of conforming his conduct at the time that he committed the crimes because he was suffering from paraphilia or, more specifically, necrophilia. The second expert witness for the defense was Dr. Judith Becker, a professor of Psychiatry and Psychology, who also diagnosed Dahmer with necrophilia.

Finally, forensic psychiatrist Dr. Carl Wahlstrom, diagnosed him with borderline personality disorder. Forensic psychiatrist Dr. Phillip Resnick for the prosecution testified that Dahmer did not suffer from primary necrophilia because he preferred live sexual partners as evidenced by his efforts to create unresistant, submissive sexual partners devoid of rational thought. He admitted that he did suffer from borderline personality disorder.

Next, Dr. Fred Fosdel, testified that, in his expert opinion, the accused was without mental disease or defect at the time he committed the murders. Rather he was a calculating and cunning murderer. He also believed he suffered from borderline personality disorder. Finally, forensic psychiatrist Dr. Park Dietz, stated that he did not believe Dahmer was suffering from any mental disease or defect at the time that he committed the crimes, adding: "Dahmer went to great lengths to be alone with his victim and to have no witnesses." He explained that there was ample evidence that Dahmer prepared in advance for each murder, therefore, his crimes were not impulsive.

He testified that his habit of becoming intoxicated prior to committing each of the murders was significant, stating: "If he had a compulsion to kill, he would not have to drink alcohol. He had to drink alcohol to overcome his inhibition, to do the crime which he would rather not do." Dr. Dietz diagnosed him with substance use disorder, paraphilia, and personality disorder not otherwise specified, with borderline and schizotypal features.

The independent expert witnesses were forensic psychiatrist Dr. George Palermo and clinical psychologist Dr. Samuel Friedman. Dr. Palermo testified that the murders were the result of a "pent-up aggression within himself. He killed those men because he wanted to kill the source of his homosexual attraction to them. In killing them, he killed what he hated in himself." He also diagnosed with borderline personality disorder.

Dr. Friedman agreed with the diagnosis of borderline personality disorder and stated that in his expert opinion it was a longing for companionship that caused Dahmer to kill, adding: "Mr. Dahmer is not psychotic." His testimony raised eyebrows in certain quarters due to his apparent sympathy for Dahmer, describing him as "amiable, pleasant to be with, courteous, with a sense of humor, conventionally handsome and charming in manner."

The jury returned their verdict on the 15 February and

determined that Dahmer was sane and not suffering from a mental disorder at the time of each of the fifteen murders for which he was tried. There were two dissenting jurors. Capital punishment was abolished in Wisconsin in 1853 so he was sentenced on the first two counts to life imprisonment plus ten years, with the remaining thirteen counts carrying a mandatory sentence of life imprisonment plus seventy years. Three months later he was extradited to Ohio where he pleaded to the murder of Hicks and was sentenced to a sixteenth term of life imprisonment.

Many experts have raised questions as to how someone who has been diagnosed as suffering from borderline personality disorder could be held to be responsible for his actions and therefore deemed sane. It's a valid question which has never been satisfactorily answered.

Because of the nature of his crimes there was always the possibility, indeed, expectation, that Jeffrey Dahmer would be subject to personal abuse and attack while serving his sentence. His first year was spent in the Columbia Correctional Institution in Portage, Wisconsin where he was initially placed in solitary confinement for his own safety. After a year, he was transferred within the Institution to a less secure unit. During this time he became a born-again Christian and in May, 1994, was baptized by Reverend Roy Ratcliff who regularly visited him and later befriended him.

He was first attacked in July, 1994, by fellow inmate, Osvoldo Durruthy, who attempted to slash his throat in the prison chapel with a razor embedded in a toothbrush. Luckily his wounds were superficial. But on the 28 November he was savagely beaten to death with a metal bar by an inmate called Christopher Scaver. Rushed to hospital he died one hour later.

9. LAWRENCE BITTAKER (1940-

"If the death penalty is not appropriate in this case, then when will it ever be?"

-Steven Kay, Prosecutor

Lawrence Bittaker is a rapist and serial killer who together with Roy Lewis Norris were known as the *Tool Box Killers*. In 1979 the pair kidnapped, raped, brutally tortured and killed five teenage girls in southern California. He is currently on death row in San Quentin State Prison awaiting execution. Despite numerous opportunities to do so, he has never expressed any regret for the suffering he inflicted upon his victims. FBI Agent, John Douglas, once described him as the most disturbing individual he ever profiled.

Lawrence didn't have much of a chance in life growing up. He was born Lawrence Sigmund on the 27 September 1940 in Pittsburgh, Pennsylvania. His biological parents put him up for adoption and he was placed in an orphanage before being adopted by George Bittaker and his wife. George worked in aircraft factories and his employment necessitated him travelling around the country. Lawrence never had the opportunity to settle anywhere and make real friends. Despite an IQ of 138 he never did well at school and was more interested in petty larceny.

His criminal career began when he was just twelve and lasted all his life. He dropped out of high school in 1957 and a year later was imprisoned at the California Youth Authority for motoring offences, hit and run and evading arrest. He remained there until he was eighteen. In the next four years he was apprehended and charged with several more minor offences. He spent eighteen months in the Oklahoma State Reformatory and later in Springfield, Missouri. Within months of his release he was sentenced to fifteen years in Los Angeles for robbery. He served two years, broke his parole and was re-arrested. The pattern continued, a never ending revolving door of crime, committal, early release and re-arrest. But each time the crimes became more serious. In fact, Bittaker spent more time in prison than out of it. In 1974 he graduated to attempted murder.

More convictions, more prison. This time while serving a sentence in San Luis Obispo, Bittaker met fellow convict Roy Norris. The pair struck up a friendship, a partnership from Hell. They became good friends and while Bittaker was later to claim in an interview with Jamie Schram in Bizarre in 2007 that he has had more sex with men than with women, he denied ever having sex with Norris. But they did share a common interest in sex and planned, on their release, to abduct, torture, rape and kill teenage girls. In fact, they fantasized about killing one girl for each teenage year from 13 through to 19. And it wasn't just prison talk.

In October 1978 Bittaker returned to Los Angeles following his release from prison. He secured employment as a skilled machinist and earned almost $1,000 per week. It was more than enough for him to put the past behind him and settle down to make something of his life. At first it seemed that this dream might become a reality. Bittaker became less introverted and integrated himself more into the community but when he discovered that his cell buddy Norris had been released from prison in January 1979 he arranged to meet up with him.

By February 1979 they had decided to put their prison fantasy plan of abduction and rape into action and acquired a van for this very purpose. They called it the

"Murder Mac." It was a 1977 GMC silver cargo van with no side windows and a large passenger sliding door. They equipped it with clothes, a cooler filled with beer, restraints, a mattress and a tool box packed with torture instruments. All they needed now were the poor unfortunate victims. Between February and June 1979 they carried out over twenty trial runs and discovered a secluded place in the San Gabriel mountains where they could bring their victims.

On the 24 June 1979 they abducted their first victim, sixteen year old Lucinda Lynn Schaeffer, from the Redondo Beach area. Once they pulled her into the van, Bittaker drove as Norris bound and gagged her. They brought her to the San Gabriel Mountains. In his account of the story Bittaker stated that Lucinda "displayed a magnificent state of self-control and composed acceptance of the conditions of which she had no control. She shed no tears, offered no resistance and expressed no great concern for her safety ... I guess she knew what was coming." Norris raped her first. Then Bittaker raped her. Norris raped her a second time. Lucinda asked Norris if they intended to kill her and if they did would they spare her "only a second, to pray." Norris told her they were not going to kill her.

After they had finished raping her Norris tried to manually strangle her but didn't succeed so Bittaker took over twisting a wire coat hanger around her neck with vice-grip pliers until her convulsions ended. They denied her the second she asked to pray. They then wrapped her body in a plastic shower curtain and threw it over a canyon to be eaten by wild animals.

On the 8 July 1978 they picked up eighteen year old Andrea Joy Hall, again in the Redondo Beach area. They lured her into the back of the vehicle where she put up a fierce fight before she was subdued. They bound and gagged her and drove to the same location as before. This time Bittaker raped her twice and Norris once. When they were finished raping her Bittaker forced her to walk, naked, up a hill alongside the road, then perform fellatio upon him. He then instructed her to pose for several Polaroid pictures. The photographs would depict her sheer terror at what had occurred. She begged for her life. Bittaker mocked her and challenged her to give him as many reasons as she could to save her life. After she ran out of reasons he thrust an ice pick through her ear and into her brain. He then thrust it into the other ear with such force that the handle broke. To ensure she was dead Bittaker strangled her and then threw her body over a cliff.

They struck again two months later, on the 3 September. The pair observed fifteen year old Jackie Doris Gilliam and thirteen year old Jacqueline Leah Lamp waiting at a bus stop near Hermosa Beach. They lured them into the van with the offer of a lift and then offered them marijuana which they accepted. When they realized that the van was not heading in the right direction an argument ensued. Norris struck Lamp on the back of the head causing her to become unconscious and then subdued Gilliam. But both girls struggled and one almost escaped before Bittaker stopped the van and helped Norris overpower the girls.

They then bound and gagged them and drove them to the mountains where they both repeatedly raped the girls over a period of two days. They even forced them to pose for pornographic photographs and made a video recording of the rapes. Bittaker tortured Jackie Gilliam by stabbing her breasts with an ice pick and using a vice grip to sever one of her nipples.

He then struck her in each ear with an ice pick puncturing her brain. Afterwards, he strangled her to death. Norris then struck Jacqueline Lamp with a sledgehammer and while Bittaker proceeded to strangle her Norris again struck her repeatedly until she died. They discarded their bodies over an embankment into the chaparral.

Approximately two months later on the 31 October they abducted their final victim, sixteen year old, part-time waitress, Shirley Lynette Ledford, from a gas station in the Sunland-Tujunga suburb of Los Angeles. They offered her a lift home and she accepted. Once inside the van Norris bound and gagged her. This time Norris drove as Bittaker insisted she scream as loud as possible. He then began striking her with a hammer, beating her breasts with his fists and using a pliers to torture her by inserting it into her vagina and rectum.

All of this occurred in between several bouts of rape and sodomy. Bittaker taped the entire incident so he could listen again and again to her terrifying pleas to stop. After an hour Bittaker and Norris changed places. Norris forced her to perform fellatio and then began striking her with the sledgehammer, breaking her bones with each strike. He struck her twenty five times on the same broken bones. After a two hour ordeal of torture Norris strangled her with a wire coat hanger, tightening it with pliers until she eventually died. They then drove to the suburbs and dumped her tortured body on the front lawn of someone's house.

Only the body of Shirley Ledford was discovered. Initially, there was nothing to connect the pair to the other murders. No one knew until in November 1979, Norris bragged about their exploits to an old acquaintance, ex-con Jimmy Dalton.

Dalton informed the Los Angeles Police Department, who advised the Redondo Beach police. Bittaker and Norris were picked up. A victim, Robin Robeck, who escaped their clutches identified them. A search of their homes provided sufficient evidence, including the tapes, to charge them with murder. Each blamed the other for the murders and eventually Norris agreed to give evidence against Bittaker in return for a life sentence. They were implicated in nineteen other murders but there was insufficient evidence to include these with the five other charges of murder.

On the 18 March, 1980, Roy Norris pleaded guilty to four counts of first-degree murder; one count of second-degree murder, two counts of rape, and one of robbery. On the 7 May, he was sentenced to forty five years to life imprisonment, with parole eligibility from 2010.

On the 24 April, 1980, Lawrence Bittaker was arraigned on a total of twenty nine charges of kidnapping, rape, sodomy and murder. His trial began on the 19 January 1981 in Torrance before Judge Thomas.

It ended on the 17 February when after deliberating for ninety minutes the jury found Bittaker guilty and he was sentenced to death for the five counts of first degree murder. Bittaker awaits execution on San Quentin's Death Row.

In the course of the trial, prosecuting attorney Steven Kay referred to the case as "one of the most shocking, brutal cases in the history of American crime." He asked the jury a poignant question: "If the death penalty is not appropriate in this case, then when will it ever be?"

Bittaker, has spent the rest of his life trying to avoid being executed.

10. RICHARD TRENTON CHASE (1950-1980)

Richard Trenton Chase known as the *Vampire of Sacramento* was an American schizophrenic serial killer who killed and cannibalized six people in four weeks in Sacramento, California and then drank their blood in the state of California in 1978.

Richard Chase was born in Santa Clara County, California on the 23 May 1950. He had one sibling, a sister who was four years younger. He was a problem child. By the age of ten he was suffering from all the symptoms commonly associated with the Macdonald triad: nocturnal enuresis, pyromania, and cruelty to animals.

By the time he was an adolescent he was already an alcoholic and a chronic drug abuser. These factors undoubtedly fueled his psychosis. Although he dated girls he was unable to sustain an erection. He constantly suffered from depression and repressed anger but no one was able to find out why. In his teens he developed hypochondria which was probably as a result of his drug addiction.

He would complain that his heart would occasionally "stop beating", or that "someone had stolen his pulmonary artery." He also believed that his cranial bones had become separated and were moving around his body. His parents asked him to move out and his father gave him the money for an apartment which he shared with various roommates.

But Richard proved impossible to live with and his flat mates came and went. They complained about his alcoholism, drug addiction, and his constant need to exhibit himself naked around the apartment. When he wouldn't leave they did. Alone in the apartment he began to bring small animals back, like cats, dogs and rabbits. He would kill them and later dissect them before eating them raw. Sometimes he would blend their organs with Coca Cola in a mixer and drink the mixture. He believed that this would prevent his heart from shrinking.

In 1975, after injecting rabbit's blood into his veins he was committed to Beverly Manor, a mental hospital for observation. Here staff caught him drinking the blood of birds. He would also defecate in his room and smear the walls with his feces. He was treated with psychotropic drugs and diagnosed as a paranoid schizophrenic. After a year of observation and treatment, he was considered not to be a risk to himself or others and was duly released. Big mistake.

With his mother's help he rented another apartment. At his stage he was definitely suffering from the classic Renfield Syndrome that is, he was addicted to drinking blood. In fact, shortly afterwards, in August, he was arrested at Pyramid Lake in Nevada sitting in his Ford Ranchero, completely naked with his body covered in blood and a bucket of blood in the boot.

The blood was not human and accordingly he was released. At this time, Bianchi and Buono were serial killers known as the *Hillside Stranglers* who were operating not far from where he lived. He became obsessed with their crimes. We will never know for sure if this was the catalyst that triggered his murder spree.

On the 29 December, 1977, fifty one year old Ambrose Griffin an engineer who was married with two children was helping his wife bring the groceries into the house from their car. Chase drove by and shot him twice, killing him instantly. No one knows why. A month later, on the 23 January he walked into the home of twenty two year old Teresa Wallin. He shot her three times. She was three months pregnant. He then raped the corpse as he stabbed it with a butcher's knife. Following the rape he savagely mutilated her. Her body was found later by her husband David Wallin.

She was lying on her back. Her legs were open and her sweater was pulled up over her breasts and her pants and underwear down around her ankles. Her torso was cut open below the sternum, and her spleen and intestines pulled out. She had been repeatedly stabbed in the lung, liver, diaphragm, and left breast. Her nipple had been completely severed. Her kidney had been cut out and placed back inside her body.

Not only had he violated her body but he had taken the trouble to collect dog feces from the garden which he had shoved into her mouth. A blood stained yoghurt carton evidence the fact that he had enjoyed her blood.

Four days later, he walked into the home of thirty eight year old Evelyn Miroth, which was situated one mile from the Wallin home He shot her friend Danny Meredith and then shot Evelyn, her six year old son Jason and two year old nephew David Ferreira. He then engaged in necrophilia with Evelyn's corpse before drinking her blood and cannibalizing her body. When a neighbor's daughter knocked on the door he fled the scene taking the body of David Ferreira with him. When police arrived at the scene they discovered perfect prints of Chase's hands and feet in Miroth's blood.

Detectives found Evelyn lying naked on the bed in her bedroom with a gunshot to the head. Her legs were open. Her stomach had been cut open and her intestines pulled out. She had been sodomized and stabbed several times through the anus into her uterus. Her neck had been slit and an attempt had been made to gouge out an eye. Her internal organs had been stabbed repeatedly. Forensic later discovered a large amount of semen in her rectum. As police looked for him, he took the baby boy David back to his home and severed his head. He removed several organs and ate them.

The FBI were called in and began to build a criminal profile of the killer. They figured him to be a white male in his mid-twenties, thin and undernourished. Evidence of the crimes, they were sure, would be found in his residence, and if he had a vehicle, in there as well. He either would have a history of mental illness or drug use, or both, and he would be something of a loner. They thought he was probably employed at some menial labor or unemployed, given his apparent state of mind, and could be receiving some disability money. He probably lived alone. He might be paranoid.

They finally tracked him down and called to his home, Apartment 15 of the Watt Avenue complex. Eventually they subdued him as he left the apartment. All through interrogation he would not admit to any crime.

They were desperate to find the missing child even though they thought he was already dead. They searched the apartment for any clues that might assist them. They were shocked at the filth and stench of the place and the fact that everything was either covered in or smeared with blood. But they had sufficient evidence to work on DNA samples which matched Chase and he was arrested and placed in custody. Police did not find the baby boy, David, until the 24 March. He had been placed in a box in a church. He was decapitated. He had been shot in the head and stabbed several times.

Chase was charged with six counts of murder. The prosecutor Ronald W. Tochterman sought the death penalty. The defense pleaded not guilty by reason of insanity. The defense sought a change of venue because the notoriety of the case would prejudice their client. The motion was granted and the case transferred one hundred and twenty miles to Santa Clara County.

Over a dozen medical experts examined the accused, Richard Chase, looking for signs of insanity. They found no evidence of any compulsion to kill. He liked blood and thought it was therapeutic. One expert said he was not schizophrenic but suffered from an antisocial personality. His thought processes were working normally and he was aware of what he had done and knew that it was wrong. Under the definition of insanity, which is based on the Macnaghten rules, Chase was legally sane.

This is the problem with the present legal definition of insanity. Simply because someone knows that what they are doing is wrong does not make them mentally competent. The law relating to insanity was devised long before advances were made in relation to mental instability and diseases. It seriously needs to be looked at afresh. In any event, the judge had no alternative but to allow the trial proceed.

In order to avoid the death penalty, his defense team tried to have him found guilty of second degree murder. This would result in a life sentence. They argued that although he might not be legally insane he was mentally unhinged and furthermore his crimes were not premeditated. It was a good defense and the best one they could come up with under the circumstances but would it work?

The highly publicized trial took four months with almost one hundred witnesses being called. Chase himself tried to explain his actions saying that he was in a comatose state. The defense argued that mentally he was clearly insane.

The prosecution argued he was a monster and a sexual sadist who knew exactly what he was doing and that it was wrong. He was sane and deserved to die.

On the 8 May, the jury, after deliberating for five hours, found Chase guilty of six counts of first degree murder. After a further four hours of discussion in relation to the appropriate penalty to be imposed, they decided that Richard Chase should be executed in the gas chamber in San Quentin.

On the 26 December, 1980, a prison guard checking cells found Chase lying awkwardly on his bed. When he opened the cell door and checked he found that the prisoner had stopped breathing. An autopsy determined that he committed suicide with an overdose of prison doctor-prescribed antidepressants that he had collected over several weeks presumably for the very purpose of committing suicide.

CHAPTER FIVE
THE TOP FIFTY SERIAL KILLERS
IN TERMS OF THE NUMBER OF KILLS

1 PEDRO LOPEZ (COLOMBIAN) 350+

Pedro Alonso Lopez aka *The Monster of the Andes* is a Colombian pedophile and rapist and probably the world's most prolific serial killer who claims to have raped and murdered in excess of 350 girls in Colombia, Ecuador and Peru between 1969 and 1980.

He was born on the 8 October 1948 in Santa Isabel, Tolima in Colombia, the seventh son of 13 children of an impoverished prostitute who later threw him out for abusing his sister. As a teen he was arrested for car theft and sentenced to 7 years in prison. He was brutally gang-raped on his second day by four older inmates. Over the next few weeks, he stabbed each one to death. Released in 1976 or 1978 he travelled to Peru where he claimed to have raped and murdered at least 100 young girls from various Indian tribes. He was caught and later deported to Ecuador. Arrested for child abduction he confessed to the murder of at least 110 girls in Ecuador, at least 100 in Colombia and "many more than 100 in Peru." All in all he was charged with 110 murders. In a secretive and swift administration of justice he was convicted in late 1980 and sentenced to life imprisonment (there being no death penalty in Ecuador.) The only interview he ever gave was to the *National Examiner's* Ray Laytner in 1999. Ray met him in a secluded and isolated part of Ambato prison where he was kept away from other prisoners. He showed no remorse for his crimes and looked forward to his freedom. He was released shortly afterwards and deported to Colombia but some commentators claim he is now living in America.

2 GARAVITO CUBILLOS (COLOMBIAN) 300+

Colombian Luis Alfredo Garavito Cubillos aka *La Bestia* (The Beast), *Tribilin* (Goofy), *El Loco* (the Crazy One) and *El Cura* (the Monk) is one of the world's most notorious and prolific pedophile and child serial sex killers with the highest confirmed number of victims at 300 and rising. He operated between 1992-1999 in Colombia and to a lesser extent in Ecuador; and his victims, with one exception, were aged between eight and thirteen. He is currently in prison but, believe it or not, he is hoping to be released in the not too distant future.

He was born in Genova, Quinido in Colombia on the 25 January 1957. He was the first born of seven boys and as a child was abused emotionally and physically by his father and sexually by two neighbors. His *modus operandi* was always the same. His targets were poor, vulnerable young boys, street urchins, aged between eight and thirteen. They were mostly street vendors. After abducting them he would get drunk, tie them up and torture them slowly savoring every moment. They were all raped and killed by at least one cut in the lateral part of the neck or by decapitation. Sometimes he would cut off their penis and stick it in their mouth. Initially 41 bodies were uncovered in the western city of Pereira in Risaralda in 1997. Twenty seven were found in neighboring Valle de Cauca. Soon bodies started appearing in sixty towns and cities in eleven out of Colombia's thirty two provinces. After an eighteen month investigation, Garavito became one of a number of suspects. He was eventually arrested on the 22 April 1999. One exhibit the police discovered was a notebook, written by him which, on 140 separate lines, contained the dates and locations of 140 separate murders. There was no formal trial. Garavito co-operated and the kill count quickly went from 140 to 182 and then passed 200. At the moment it stand at just over 300 murders.

3 DR. HAROLD SHIPMAN (BRITISH) 250+

Harold Fredrick Shipman aka *Doctor Death* is probably one of the most prolific serial killers in recorded history. Although only convicted of fifteen murders it is generally accepted that his total tally was in excess of two hundred and fifty and possibly as high as four hundred. He was a British medical practitioner who executed his patients by lethal injection.

He was born on the 14 January 1946 in Nottingham, England, the middle child of working class and devout Methodist parents. He was particularly close to his mother and was 17 when she died of lung cancer on the 21 June 1963. The incident prompted him to become a doctor. He married Primrose Oxtoby on the 5 November 1966 and studied medicine at Leeds School of Medicine graduating in 1970. In 1993 he founded his own surgery at 21 Market Street in Hyde. He was a typical organized killer who operated a single *modus operandi*. Many were elderly women, like his mother. He preferred to visit his victims in their homes. None or very few of his patients, when attended by him, were in perfect health so being treated by him at the time of their death would not necessarily have raised suspicions. However, what did raise suspicions was the sheer volume of deaths that occurred. Shipman was arrested on the 7 September 1998. When questioned, Shipman denied responsibility for any of the deaths. He continuously lied to the police, his patients and their next of kin. He falsified medical reports and death certificates in an attempt to back up the cause of death. His trial began on the 5 October 1999 and on 31 January 2000, the jury found him guilty of fifteen murders. Later, the Shipman Inquiry concluded he was probably responsible for about 250 deaths. At 6:10 a.m. on the 13 January 2004, on the eve of his fifty eight birthday, Harold Shipman committed suicide by hanging in his cell at Wakefield Prison.

4 HENRY LEE LUCAS (AMERICAN) 150-200

Lucas aka *The Deadly Drifter* is one of America's most infamous depraved sexual deviants and serial killers. Initially, he confessed to six hundred murders but the authorities seriously doubted this claim. In March 1985 they stated that the fully verified murders attributable to Lucas alone was ninety, covering twenty states while Lucas and Ottis Toole, as a murder partnership, were responsible for a further one hundred and eight, later to increase to over two hundred. Lucas eventually recanted his confessions. He claimed that all he was trying to do was improve his jail conditions. He then asserted that he really only ever killed one person, his dear old momma, Viola.

Henry was born on the 23 August 1936 at Blacksburg, Virginia, into a dysfunctional and destitute family. His mother, Viola, was a prostitute who regularly turned tricks in her home in front of her husband and two boys. In 1954 he was convicted of numerous counts of burglary and received a sentence of six years in prison. Twice he escaped; twice he was re-captured. On the 11 January 1960, following a drunken argument, he stabbed his mother in the neck with a knife. He then fled the scene, was arrested, tried and sentenced to twenty to forty years in prison. He was released after ten years. In 1976, the forty year old, one eyed, bisexual Lucas teamed up with the twenty nine year old, homosexual arsonist and degenerate serial killer, depraved Ottis Elwood Toole. They first met in a rescue mission for down and outs in Jacksonville. It was to prove to be a match made in hell. They traveled through a minimum of twenty six states, with Lucas targeting female hitchhikers and Toole preying on males. Eventually, Lucas was arrested on the 11 June 1983 on a charge of being an ex-convict who possessed a handgun. He was held in custody and later was to make the sensational claims of hundreds of killings.

5 COUNTESS BATHORY (HUNGARY) 150+

Countess Erzsebet (Elizabeth) Báthory de Ecsed aka the *Blood Countess* is regarded by many scholars as the most prolific female serial killer in history. Convicted of eighty murders, her final count is reputed to be in excess of six hundred. But as she always had at least four accomplices her total tally has been divided by four to give a kill count of 150 making her by far the worst female serial killer in history. Her victims were mostly young peasant girls until she began killing young women of noble stock. She enjoyed torturing her victims over a period of days before they finally died.

She was born on the 8 August 1560 in Nyirbator, a town in north east Hungary. Her father was George Báthory while her mother, Anna Báthory, was related to the Hungarian noble Stefan Báthory who was King of Poland and Duke of Transylvania. She was engaged to Ferenc Nádasdy at the age of twelve. They married on the 8 May 1575 at the Palace of Varannó in front of 4,500 guests. It is not known for certain when Elizabeth began torturing young peasant girls as a past-time. But there is no doubt that she, and her accomplices, tortured hundreds of girls for their own sadistic pleasure. They then began murdering young girls of noble birth. Whatever about the murder of peasants the murder of nobles could not be countenanced. The King of Hungary ordered her arrest. The show trials of her accomplices took place in January 1611 where they confessed to their heinous crimes in a matter of days, probably having been tortured first. In a second trial, another servant, Zusanna, gave evidence of the existence of a register where Elizabeth had overseen the deaths of six hundred and fifty young girls. The entries were in Elizabeth's handwriting. Her accomplices were executed. She attended neither trial and was simply placed under house arrest until her death in 1614.

6 DANIEL BARBOSA (COLOMBIAN) 150+

Daniel Camargo Barbosa killed and raped over one hundred and fifty young girls in Colombia and Ecuador during the 1970s and 1980s before being murdered in prison. He was tried on a single count to ensure a conviction and sentenced to thirty years on the prison island of Gorgona, known as the Colombian Alcatraz. He escaped in 1984 and travelled to Ecuador where most of the murders took place. He was captured in Quito in 1986 where he confessed to killing seventy one girls since his escape. In 1989 he received the maximum sentence available in Ecuador. This was a mere sixteen years. In November 1994 he was murdered in prison.

He was born in Bogota in Colombia on the 22 January 1936 to dysfunctional parents. His first serious conviction in Colombia, for sexual assault, was on the 10 April 1964 and he was sentenced to three years in prison, later increased to eight years. Furious at the increase in sentence he vowed vengeance on his release. He took out his revenge by kidnapping a random nine year old school girl whom he raped and murdered. He was convicted and sentenced to thirty years, later reduced to twenty five, which he was to spend on the prison island of Gorgona, known as the Colombian Alcatraz. In November 1984 he escaped and travelled to Ecuador where between 1984-1986 he raped and murdered at least 50 children. He was eventually captured in Quito on the 26 February 1986. When interrogated he calmly confessed to killing seventy one girls in Ecuador since his escape from Gorgona and showed no remorse. He later led authorities to where he had dumped the bodies not yet accounted for. He admitted to raping his victims before hacking them to bits with a machete. He chose young virgins because he liked to hear them cry. His motivation for killing women was that he hated them because they were always unfaithful.

7 DARYA SALTYKOVA (RUSSIAN) 138

Darya Nikolayevna Saltykova was convicted of the torture and murder of one hundred and thirty eight of her servants mostly women and young girls. Saltykova was commonly known as Saltychikha. That name was to become a synonym for the bestial treatment of peasants in pre-reformation Russia.

She was born Daria Ivanova on the 3 November 1730 in Moscow. Her parents were Nikolai Avtonomovich Ivanov and Anna Ivanovna Ivanov. At an early age the family arranged for her to marry into the noble and famous Russian family, the Saltykovs. She married Glebovich Aleksejevich Saltykov whose father was Alexei Petrovich Saltykov, a Russian boyar and governor of Moscow and Kazan. Her husband Glebovich died unexpectedly when she was just twenty six leaving her the richest widow in Moscow. On his death she inherited Troitskoe, a beautiful estate near Moscow where she lived with her three young sons and over five hundred serfs. She also inherited other valuable property in Moscow. She then began to torture and murder her serfs. The families of the victims complained to the authorities and eventually aristocrat Countess Elizabeth Báthory de Ecsed was warned. But the complaints continued and the savagery escalated to such an extent that eventually a petition was submitted to Empress Catherine II. Saltychikha was arrested in 1762. She was held for six years while the authorities conducted an investigation. She was found to have murdered one hundred and thirty six women and children and three men. Finally, six years after she was arrested, she was sentenced on the 2 October 1768, to life imprisonment in the Ivanovsky Cloister. She died in her cell on the 27 November, 1801, at the age of seventy one after thirty three years of incarceration. She was buried in her family's grave in Donskoy Monastery.

8 DR. H. H. HOLMES (AMERICAN) 100+

Dr. Henry Howard Holmes aka the *Beast of Chicago* is one of the America's first documented serial killers in the modern sense of the word. The ultimate lady killer, Holmes is credited with a confirmed kill count of twenty seven but it is generally accepted that his real body count was well in excess of one hundred. Recent evidence, physical and forensic, which was uncovered in 2013, suggests that there is a growing likelihood that he was also the infamous *Jack the Ripper*. Holmes was actually born Herman Webster Mudgett but changed his name to avoid detection in a number of insurance scams. He is one of America's most prolific serial killer.

He was born on the 16 May 1861 in Gilmanton, New Hampshire to Levi Horton Mudgett and his wife, Theodate Page Price. He attended Michigan Medical School and thus began his life of crime. In 1888 in Chicago he began building what was later to be called the Murder Castle, a development with retail shops and hotel accommodation. No one knows for certain just how many hotel visitors were lured to their death by the evil Dr. Holmes in his Castle of Horrors but the indications are that at least 100 were murdered by him. He later burned it down in an attempt to collect the insurance but they refused to pay. He married several times and murdered most of his wives after conning them out of whatever money they had. He was eventually caught after being on the run for several months and was tried for murder. He was convicted and sentenced to be hanged. He claimed to have killed over 100 people but he later amended this to 27. It seemed as if he would pluck the figures out of thin air. On May 7, 1896, Holmes was hanged at Moyamensing Prison, in Philadelphia. When his neck did not properly snap he was slowly strangled to death and pronounced dead after twenty minutes.

9 TED BUNDY (AMERICAN) 100-

Theodore Robert Bundy is known to have tortured raped and murdered a minimum of thirty six young women between 1974 and 1978 but his actual total kill count is estimated at just shy of one hundred. Born Theodore Robert Cowell, he had the ability, charisma and drive to become the Republican Governor of the State of Washington but he ended up being executed in the electric chair at Raiford Prison in Starke, Florida, on the 24 January 1989 at the age of forty two. He was one of America's most cold, sadistic, and psychopathic killers.

He was born to Eleanor Louise Cowell in Burlington Vermont on the 24 November 1946. He never knew his father. Throughout his entire life Bundy was a pathological liar and a kleptomaniac who would steal anything that wasn't nailed down. No one knows for certain when Ted Bundy began killing beautiful young women but it was definitely as early as 1969 and maybe even 1961. He began killing in earnest in 1974. Most of his victims were young, white, beautiful women with long brown hair. His *modus operandi* was that he would pretend to be injured and ask them for assistance. He lured them to his car, abducted them and brought them to a place to torture them. He raped them before killing and would often return to have sex with the corpse. He began his first killing campaign in Washington, Oregon. College students went missing at the rate of one per month. He also killed in Utah, Florida and Colorado. He was charged with several murders in different states and sentenced to death. Immediately thereafter, Bundy began a long series of appeals all of which failed. In his eleventh hour, he decided to confess to more crimes with a now official death count of thirty six. Both Ann Rule and Dr. Bob Keppel who both wrote extensively about Bundy, believe that Bundy was most likely responsible for the deaths of at least 100 women.

10 GARY RIDGWAY (AMERICAN) 80+

On the 5 November 2003, Ridgway entered a guilty plea to forty eight charges of aggravated first degree murder as part of a plea bargain, agreeing that in return for a life sentence he would co-operate in locating the remains of his victims. He was sentenced to life without parole and will never be released. His notoriety lies in the fact that he confessed to more confirmed murders than any other American serial killer. Initially he admitted responsibility for the deaths of sixty five women and later seventy one. He claimed that they were all killed in King County, hoping that prosecutors outside King County would not try to have him executed. But speculation is rife that Ridgway killed many more and buried them outside of King County.

Gary Leon Ridgway was born in Salt Lake City, Utah, to Mary Rita Steinman and Thomas Newton Ridgway on the 18 February 1949. He had two brothers, Gregory Leon and Thomas Edward. He suffered a troubled childhood with a domineering mother and a set of parents who constantly argued. But with a poor education and little prospects he decided to join the navy and was dispatched to Vietnam, where he served on board a supply ship and saw combat. It was during his time in the military that Ridgway developed an appetite for prostitutes. His insistence on having unprotected sex resulted in him contracting gonorrhea. The disease so angered him that he developed an intense hatred for all prostitutes. He was eventually caught many years after his crimes through DNA evidence. He was arrested on four counts of aggravated murder but on the 5 November 2003, he entered a guilty plea to forty eight charges of aggravated first degree murders as part of a plea bargain organized by his counsel, Anthony Savage. However, his kill count is suspected to be considerably higher.

11 SERHIY TKACH (UKRAINE) 36-130

Serhiy Fedorovich Tkach aka the *Pologovsky Maniac* is a Ukrainian serial killer who was convicted of the rape and killing of 36 women and girls between 1980 and 2005. A cruel and sadistic necrophiliac, he himself claimed to have killed approximately 130 women.

Serhiy was born on the 15 September 1952 in Kiselyovsk, in the Russian SFSR. Very little is known about his life. He was married three times and had four children. However, it is known that he was a former Ukrainian police criminal investigator who was a forensic expert and that he was originally from Russia. He carefully planned his killings and skillfully avoided leaving scene of crime evidence. He worked as a police investigator in Siberia for many years, learning all the police procedures and forensic science. Later he utilized this expertise to evade capture long enough to claim victim after victim. After his time with the police force, Tkach moved to the Ukraine, making his way by working in coal mines and industrial plants. This was when his killing spree most likely began. It wasn't until a witness saw him in the company of a friend's daughter, who later disappeared and was murdered, that he was finally caught in 2005.

Most of his victims were between the ages of eight and eighteen. He sexually tortured them before suffocating them. He is known to have also sexually abused their bodies after death. When caught he admitted his crimes and demanded that he be sentenced to death. He was tried for the rape and murder of thirty six women in a tribunal in Dnipropetrovsk a city in southeastern Ukraine, and after a year-long investigation he was sentenced to life imprisonment. He is in custody in an undisclosed high security prison. Several people were wrongly convicted and imprisoned for his crimes with some committing suicide.

12 ALBERT H. FISH (AMERICAN) 23-100

Albert Hamilton Fish known as *The Grey Man* was a sexual pervert, sadist, cannibal, child killer and probably American's most infamous serial killer ever. He claimed to have tortured, mutilated and killed at least one child in every American State before his eventual capture. He ate the bodies of many of his victims. He claimed he had "done" one hundred children.

He was born on the 19 May, 1870, in Washington, D.C. into a middle class family. His father was Captain Randall Fish, a Potomac River boat captain who later made and sold fertilizer. His mother, Ellen, was of Scots-Irish ancestry. His father was forty three years older than his mother and was seventy five when Albert was born. He had three siblings who lived, Walter, Annie and Edwin. His father dropped dead on the 15 October 1875 from myocardial infarction.

Fish began molesting children, mostly young boys, as early as 1890 and engaged in every type of sexual perversion known to man including urolagnia, drinking urine and coprophagia, eating feces. Although he was based in New York his painting business took him elsewhere and he travelled around extensively. When he was under suspicion he would simply move on to another state and another child. But it was the high profile abductions of Grace Budd, Francis McDonnell and Billy Gaffney that would eventually lead to his downfall. He was arrested on the 13 December 1934 and while in custody made a full and rank statement confessing to a number of murders and was sentenced to death. Less than a year after his trial, Hamilton Albert Fish ate his last meal. Shortly after 11:00 p.m. on the 16 January, 1936 Fish was strapped into the chair and executed by Robert Elliott the official executioner, another grey man.

13 RICHARD COTTINGHAM (AMERICAN) 7-100

Richard Cottingham, the *Torso Killer* is an American serial sex killer and sadist who savaged to death a minimum of seven young women in the New York area between 1967 and 1980 but is believed to have killed close to one hundred others.

He was born on the 25 November 1946 in the Bronx, New York City, the first born of three children. His parents were respectable middle class people. At eighteen he left Valley High and worked for father's insurance company Metropolitan Life as a computer operator. In 1966 he moved to Blue Cross Blue Shield of Greater New York as a computer operator. Nobody knows what turned this quiet computer operator from a respectable young man into a sadist and serial sex killer. There was no history of juvenile crime, enuresis, arson or animal torture when he was growing up. But he began a campaign of rape, torture and murder in 1967 at the age of twenty one.

Outwardly, Richard Cottingham, seemed to have it all; a loving wife, three beautiful children, a good job and a detached house. Inside the depraved mind of Richard Cottingham lurked a sexually violent man obsessed with control, bondage and sexual sadism. From August 1980 he was charged with various murders in various states and convicted in all cases. He received numerous life sentences and remains in prison to this day. Far from being remorseful for his crimes he constantly brags about how good he was as a serial killer. Cottingham drugged, abducted and tortured dozens of girls. He didn't care if they lived or died. He derived his pleasure from the torture he inflicted, not from the killings. In his one only ever media interview he claimed to have killed almost one hundred women and that his ambition had always been to be the best serial killer ever.

14 RODNEY ALCALA (AMERICAN) 7-100

Rodney Alcala known as the *Dating Game Killer* was an American serial killer and rapist who was active between 1971-1979. He was convicted of seven murders but was suspected of killing up to one hundred women. He was born Rodrigo Jacques Alcala Buquor in San Antonio, Texas in 1943. His parents were Raoul Alcala Buquor and Anna Maria Guitierrez. Considered to be highly intelligent Rodney graduated from UCLA School of Fine Arts. In 1968 he raped and beat an 8 year old girl with a steel bar. He evaded capture and fled to New York where he enrolled in NYU Film School. In 1971 he raped and murdered Cornelia Michel Crilly, a twenty three year old Flight Attendant in her Manhattan apartment, again avoiding capture. But his luck ran out when two students at a New Hampshire camp recognized his face on an FBI Wanted posted. He was extradited back to California, convicted of assault and paroled after seventeen months.

Within two months he was arrested again, this time for sexually assaulting a thirteen year old girl. Once again, he was released early and served only two years. His parole officer allowed him fly to New York where, within one week, he was suspected of killing twenty three year old Ellen Jane Hover. He returned to Los Angeles and in 1980 was arrested and tried for the murder of twelve year old Robin Samsoe. He was convicted and sentenced to death but his conviction was overturned. He was re-tried, re-convicted and once again sentenced to death. And, incredibly, his conviction was, once again, overturned. Later he was indicted for the murder of four additional women. He was found guilty and sentenced to death. In 2011 he was indicted for two more murders, pleaded guilty and was sentenced to twenty five years to life. Despite his seven murders he is suspected of committing a minimum of 100 other murders.

15 JOHN BODKIN ADAMS (BRITISH) 0-160

John Bodkin Adams was a Northern Irish medical practitioner, a convicted fraudster and a suspected serial killer. He was only ever charged with one murder and was acquitted of that. But the fact is that between 1946 and 1956 more than 160 of his patients died in suspicious circumstances and of these 132 left him something in their wills. Some scholars consider him to be the forerunner of mass murderer Dr. Harold Shipman (qv), while others believe that all he was ever guilty of was carrying out mercy killings at a time when painkillers were the only option to alleviate terminal illness.

Adams was born in Randalstown in Country Antrim, Northern Ireland on the 21 January 1899 to Samuel Adams and Ellen Bodkin. He was educated at Queens University in Belfast from which he qualified as a doctor in 1921. In 1922 he joined a general practitioner's practice in Eastbourne, Sussex in England. By 1935 serious rumors began circulating about Dr. Adams' unconventional methods after a patient, Matilda Whitton, left him £7,385 in her will. By 1956 he was one of the wealthiest doctors in Britain. The fact that he had been the beneficiary of over one hundred testamentary bequests may have helped. But rumors turned to suspicion and he was eventually tried for murder and acquitted in a trial that was plagued with political interference. In 2003 police archives were opened at the request of historian Pamela Cullen, who believes that Adams "may have had more victims than Shipman." She says that Adams was acquitted due to the way the case was prosecuted rather that Adams' lack of guilt.

Author John Emsley says: "It now seems almost certain that over a thirty year period he killed one hundred and sixty of his patients." Dr. John Bodkin Adams died on the 4 July 1983 in Eastbourne leaving £402,970.

16 VOLKER ECKERT (GERMAN) 13-80

Volker Eckert aka the *Brummi Killer* was a German serial killer who murdered at least thirteen women and probably as many as eighty while driving a truck though Europe. He targeted prostitutes and down and outs, and had sex with them before strangling them. He then took Polaroid photographs of their dead bodies as well as trophies like locks of hair, trinkets and parts of their clothing.

Volker Eckert was born in Plauen, then East Germany in 1959. As a young boy he developed a pathological liking to long hair and liked to stroke his sisters' doll's hair and later his mother's hairpiece while masturbating. At night he would wander the dark street of Plauen seeking out street prostitutes to attack. From 1978 to 1986 it is believed that he attacked at least thirty women in Plauen. He received several convictions for assault and served a number of prison sentences. On his release he moved to Hof in West Germany. In 1999, when he was forty Eckert qualified as a long-distance lorry driver which provided him with the opportunity to kill at will throughout Europe. Killing in one country and returning to another is the optimum way to avoid detection. He was arrested on the 17 November 2006 in Cologne and confessed after one hour. In his flat police found numerous Polaroid photographs of dead women. Volker Eckert had written notes on the back of each photograph indicating how he had killed them. To this day many of those women remain unidentified. Underneath his bed they found a life size rubber doll. The doll was decorated with trophies collected from his victims.

On the 1 July 2007, Eckert committed suicide in his cell. It was his forty eight birthday. In addition to the thirteen murders referred to in this biography he was directly connected to a minimum of thirty two others.

17 PEDRO FILHO (BRAZILIAN) 71+

Pedro Rodrigues Filho aka *Pedrinho Matador* is a notorious Brazilian vigilante multiple killer known to be responsible for a minimum of seventy one murders. He was born on a farm in 1954 in Santa Rita do Sapucaí, south of Minas Gerais in Brazil to Pedro and Manuela Filho. When he was 14, incensed that his father had been wrongly sacked as school guard for stealing food from the school kitchen, he attacked and killed Minas Gerais the vice-Mayor of Alfenas. He then murdered another guard who was apparently the real culprit and fled to São Paulo where he became involved in drug trafficking, torture and murder. By the time he had reached his eighteenth birthday he had already murdered ten people. Following an argument, his father killed his mother by stabbing her twenty one times. Filho retaliated by hacking his father to death with a machete and ripping out his heart, biting a chunk out of it and spitting it out.

In May 1973 he was arrested, charged with robbery, drug trafficking and multiple murders and sent to prison in Araquara in Sao Paulo. There, with the use of body building and steroids, he became a virtual killing machine and murdered forty seven inmates and guards. He was eventually released by the authorities on the 24 April 2007 after which he went to Fortaleza in Ceará in the north east of Brazil. On his release he helped instigate six riots and gained notoriety after making a promise to murder serial killer Francisco de Assisi Pereira, aka *The Park Maniac*, who strangled several people in Sao Paulo. He became something of a political activist and on the 15 September, 2011, he was arrested by police for riot and false imprisonment at Balneário Camboriú, Santa Catarina and returned to prison. Although not strictly speaking a serial killer in the pure meaning of the term, Filho is certainly Brazil's most notorious killer.

18 GARY RIDGWAY (AMERICAN) 49-71

Gary Leon Ridgway aka the *Green River Killer* is an American serial killer who was initially convicted of 48 separate murders. Ridgway murdered numerous women and girls, mostly prostitutes, in Washington State during the 1980s and 1990s. His *modus operandi* involved strangling the women and dumping their bodies in rivers or throughout forested and overgrown areas in King County, often returning to the dead bodies to have sexual intercourse with them.

He was born in Salt Lake City, Utah, to Mary Rita Steinman and Thomas Newton Ridgway on the 18 February 1949. He suffered a troubled childhood and had a low IQ. He joined the US army and saw action in Vietnam. Here he developed an appetite for, and then deep hatred of, prostitutes. Back at home his wife Claudia, alone and bored, left him. He later remarried a girl called Marcia Winslow but this second marriage also ended in divorce due largely to infidelity. It was during this second marriage that Ridgway found religion. Meanwhile, Ridgway was obsessed with sex demanding it from his wife several times each day. He was finally arrested on the 30 November 2001 for the murders of four women whose cases were linked to him through DNA evidence. As part of a plea bargain wherein he agreed to disclose the whereabouts of still-missing women, he was spared the death penalty and received a sentence of life imprisonment without parole. Over a five month period, Ridgway confessed to 48 murders, more confirmed murders than any other American serial killer. At one stage he told investigators he murdered 65 women later increased to 71 women and confessed to having had sex with them before killing them, a detail which he did not reveal until after his sentencing. He is incarcerated at Washington State Penitentiary in Walla Walla, Washington, America.

19 FRITS HAARMAN (GERMAN) 24-70

Friedrich Heinrich Karl "Frits" Haarmann aka *The Butcher of Hanover* aka *The Vampire of Hanover* is Germany's most notorious serial sex killer. A homosexual pedophile, cannibal and killer, Haarmann raped, tortured and killed a minimum of twenty four young men in post-war Germany. Although convicted of only twenty four murders he himself claimed to have killed between fifty and seventy young men. Along with Peter Kurten and Carl Großmann he was one of the inspirations for the protagonist, Hans Becker (played by Peter Lorre) in Fritz Lang's classic German film *M*.

Haarmann was born on the 25 October 1879 in Hanover. He was the youngest child of Ollie Haarmann ("Sulky Ollie") and Johanna Claudius. Johanna came from a wealthy family and received a rich dowry on her marriage. Frits grew up to be a weak, effeminate young boy who hated his father. He joined the army twice but operated mostly as a petty criminal and received several short sentences before receiving an eight year stretch for robbery. Released in 1918 he became a paid police informer. Even as this stage Haarmann was known to be a homosexual who lured unsuspecting young boys back to his apartment for sex. Most were runaways, drifters, urchins or new arrivals to a city plagued by decadence, destruction and decay. After his arrest he made a full, if somewhat less than frank, confession. In the six years between 1918-1924 he claimed to have murdered a minimum of 24 young men but at one stage also claimed he had murdered between 50-70. On the 19 December 1924, Haarmann was found guilty of all but three of the murders and sentenced to death. No appeal was made in relation to the sentence and on the 15 April 1925 he was beheaded by guillotine by a relative of Magdeburg executioner, Carl Gröpler.

20 RANDY KRAFT (AMERICAN) 16-70

Randolph "Randy" Steven Kraft aka *The Scorecard Killer* aka *The Freeway Killer* had the charm, good looks, political savvy, work ethos, intelligence and ambition to have become a Republican Senator. But at the age of nineteen, while in his second year of study for a Bachelor of Arts degree in Economics at Claremont Men's College, Kraft's life went suddenly off the rails. Instead, he ended up as just another notorious American rapist, sexual sadist and serial killer responsible for the torture and murder of a minimum of sixteen young men; but his final total is more likely to shave the seventy mark. He is currently incarcerated on death row in San Quentin State Prison.

He was born on the 19 March 1945 and when he was three the family moved to Midway City in Orange County. A gifted student, Randy struggled with his sexuality and having "come out" felt that his family abandoned him. He went to college and then joined the US Air Force but it all went downhill after that. Randy by name and randy by nature he would cruise the gay bars every night seeking one night stands. He had a preference for Marines but basically anyone would do. The sex escalated to sex with violence, torture, murder and ultimately depravity. Between 1971 and 1983 he raped and murdered almost seventy young men. The majority of murders took place in California although at least six were killed in Oregon and two in Michigan. All of his victims were mostly aged between eighteen and twenty five. Many were enlisted in the Marines. He was initially charged with just 16 murders and sentenced to death on the 29 November 1989. Kraft is right up there as one of America's most prolific and sadistic serial killers of all time. However, for some inexplicable reason he has not received the notoriety his heinous crimes deserve. He is now in custody thirty one years, fifteen on Death Row. He is a model prisoner.

21 ALEX PICHUSHKIN (RUSSIAN) 48-63

Alexander "Saha Pichushkin aka the *Bitsa Park Maniac* and later the *Chessboard Killer* was convicted of 48 murders but insisted he had killed 63. He conducted his killing campaign in Moscow between 2001 and 2006. He was born on the 9 April 1974 in Mytishci, Moscow Oblast. His father abandoned the family soon after he was born and it was up to his mother, the diminutive Natasha Pichushkin, to look after the young boy and his half-sister, Katya. Natasha moved into her home, a two bed apartment on the fifth floor of 2 Khersonskaya in a south Moscow suburb when she was eleven and lived there all her life. The apartment is situated in a lower middle class part of Moscow six minutes from the north end of Bitsevsky Park.

When Pichushkin was arrested police confirmed that the thirty two year old supermarket assistant slept in the front bedroom on a couch which doubled as a sitting room. His ageing mother slept in a bed ten feet away. The second bedroom was occupied by his half-sister, twenty seven year old, Katya, her husband, also called Alexander, and their six year old son Sergei. Sasha was not an extraordinary Russian. He drank too much, he smoked too much, he had a menial job, he was rough, crude and had no hope for the future. He had no girlfriend and no prospects but he was a gifted champion chess player. On the 11 May 2001 he killed Yevgeny Pronin. It was to be the start of a five year murder spree. In fact, over the next eight weeks he killed nine people; and that fall and winter five more, mostly elderly men who were his neighbors. He was arrested in June 2006, confessed and was convicted on the 24 October 2007 of forty nine murders and three attempted murders.

He was sentenced by Judge Vladimir Usov to life in prison with the first fifteen years in solitary confinement.

22 TOMMY LYNN SELLS (AMERICAN) 1-70

The case of American psychopath and serial killer Tommy Lynn Sells, a sexual predator who stalked, raped and murdered women and young girls is disturbing on a number of levels. Sells aka the *Coast-to-Coast Killer* was a drug-addicted drifter who was convicted of one murder, linked to fifteen and claimed seventy during the period 1980 to 1999. He targeted mothers and their young daughters and his crimes are particularly heinous. He was sentenced to death and executed on the 3 April 2014 after the failure of his lawyers to obtain a postponement.

Sells and his twin sister, Tammy Jean, were born on the 28 June 1964 in Kingsport, Tennessee to a neglectful mother, Nina Sells. He never knew his father. Sexually abused as a child, by the age of fourteen he was a tear-away who experimented with alcohol and drugs and ran away from home and just drifted. Between 1978 and 1999 he travelled across several states, and when he wasn't doing odd jobs he was thieving, raping and eventually killing. It was typical of the type of confession he would make when he was arrested. He claimed he had killed seventy people but after the Henry Lee Lucas (qv) debacle police were now reluctant to accept the word of a serial killer.

He committed many despicable crimes including a particularly depraved multiple homicide in 1987 in Illinois when he massacred the Dardeen family, including a three year old boy, a pregnant wife and her newly born baby. It took the police twelve years to find the perpetrator of this heinous crime.

After fourteen years on death row in the Allan B. Polunsky Unit near Livingston, Texas, Tommy Lynn Sells was eventually executed on the 3 April 2014. He is regarded as one of Texas' most violent and dangerous offenders.

23 MARCEL A. PETIOT (FRENCH) 26-60

Dr. Marcel Petiot aka the *Butcher of Paris* is one of France's most notorious serial killers who was convicted of twenty six murders but is credited with killing at least sixty people for profit in wartime France.

He was born Marcel André Henri Félix Petiot on the 17 January 1897 in Auxerre in France. Later, he was sent to school in Paris. After schooling he joined the French infantry and was dispatched to the front in November 1916. In March 1919, he was admitted to a psychiatric hospital in Rennes. At the time, war veterans were afforded the opportunity to enroll in an accelerated education program and Petiot chose medicine. Notwithstanding his mental instability, he completed his medical school training in less than a year, serving a two-year psychiatric internship.

On the 15 December 1921 he receive his full degree from the *Faculté de Médeceine de Paris* and later moved to Villeneuve-sur-Yonne where the dashing twenty five year old doctor set up his own practice, entered politics, was fined and imprisoned and eventually moved to Paris in 1933. In 1936 he was appointed *médecin d'etat-civil* for the 9th arrondissement of Paris which afforded him greater opportunities for his criminal activities. At the beginning of the World War II he devised a bogus scheme offering an escape route out of France and having fleeced the participants he murdered them and burned their bodies in his home. At his celebrated trial for 27 murders he claimed he was a member of the Resistance and that they were enemies of France. The trial was the OJ Simpson case of the time and was front page news in every European country. Zero or Hero? After just deliberating for a mere three hours, the jury found him guilty of 26 premeditated murders and he was sentenced to death.

24 ANATOLY ONOPRIENKO (UKRAINE) 52

Anatoly Yuriyovych Onoprienko aka *The Terminator*, *Citizen O* and *The Beast of Ukraine* was a notorious Ukrainian serial killer who murdered fifty two people over a six year period. He was born on the 25 July 1959 in Lasky in Zhytomyr Oblast. His father, Yuri, was a decorated war hero and when his mother died, he was sent to an orphanage in Privitnoe. On his release and with no proper education or skills he turned to a life of crime. Initially this involved burglary but this soon graduated to murder.

His *modus operandi* was to select a house in an isolated area. Rather than quietly rob the house he would cause a commotion to alert the occupants. When confronted he would first kill the adult male and then his spouse before finishing off the children. In order to destroy any evidence he usually set the house on fire. Anyone unfortunate enough to witness the attack would also be eliminated. He was eventually apprehended in May 1996 by the SBU, Security Serive Ukraine. Initially, he confessed to eight killings but later he increased this to fifty two murders. He claimed to have been instructed to kill by voices in his head. However, psychiatrists deemed him stable enough to stand trial.

During the trial he was confined to a metal cage in the body of the Court and frequently clashed with the judge. At one stage the judge refused his request to have his attorney changed from the state appointed attorney, Ruslan Mashkovsky, to another lawyer who is "at least 50 years old, Jewish or half-Jewish, economically independent and has international experience." Because of his country's entry into the Council of Europe he escaped the death penalty even though he was sentenced to death. He died of a heart attack on the 27 August 2013 while serving his sentence at a prison in Zhytomyr.

25 DONALD HARVEY (AMERICAN) 28-57

Hospital orderly Donald Harvey is an American serial often referred to as the *Angel of Death*, who as a nurse managed to murder a minimum of thirty seven and possibly fifty seven patients over a period of seventeen years primarily in the Marymount Hospital in London, Kentucky, the Cincinnati V.A. Medical Hospital, and Cincinnati's Drake Memorial Hospital. He is currently prisoner number JC0404989 at the Allen Correctional Institution in Lima, Ohio.

Donald was born on the 15 April, 1952 in Butler County, Ohio into a comfortable middle class family. He was the first of three children. Shortly after his birth the family moved to Booneville, Kentucky. A comfortable background, a decent education, a loving family, Donald had none of the problems associated with serial killers while growing up. But he did have some serious hang-ups and psychological issues which appear never to have been properly addressed.

By 18 he was working at the Marymount Hospital in London, Kentucky. While there he became addicted to marijuana. He worked there for just ten months but later claimed that within that short period he murdered a minimum of twelve patients. When not poisoning or killing patients, he took his anger out on anyone else who annoyed him. He poisoned his lover, Carl Hoeweler, two of his neighbors, Diane Alexander and Helen Metzger, as well as his lover's father, Henry Hoeweler. In 1975 he was a nursing assistant at the VA Hospital in Lexington. Several patients died in suspicious circumstances while he was there. The following year he began working at Daniel Drake Memorial in Cincinnati, Ohio where he began killing again. He was brought in for questioning and confessed to all his murders to avoid the death penalty.

26 ANDREI CHIKATILO (UKRAINE) 52+

Andrei Chikatilo, the *Butcher of Rostov*, was the Soviet Union's most notorious serial sex killer, responsible for the mutilation and murder of at least fifty two women and children between 1978 and 1990 in Russian SFSR, the Ukrainian SSR and the Uzbek SSR.

He was born on the 16 October 1936 in Yabluchne in the Ukrainian SSR. His parents, Roman and Anna, were extremely poor co-operative farm laborers who lived in a one-room house and barely had sufficient food to survive. He was drafted into the Soviet Army in 1957. He was assigned to a KGB communications unit in Berlin and later joined the Communist party in 1960. In 1963, Chikatilo wed Feodosia Odnacheva. In 1970, Chikatilo began working as a teacher and in 1978 began his killing campaign.

In 1984 he had already killed fifteen people when he stopped. But by 1987 he had resumed and killed three more on business trips away from the Rostov Oblast. In early 1988, he killed another three people and then a further four. It wasn't until the 20 November 1990 he was arrested and interrogated. He eventually confessed after ten days. His trial, which began on the 14 April 1992, was the first major media event of the newly liberalized post-Soviet Russia. Proceedings commenced in Rostov on 14 April 1992. During the trial, he was kept in an iron cage to protect him from attacks by the victims' relatives. He was often removed due to him continuously interrupting the trial, exposing himself, singing, and refusing to answer questions. On the 15 October, he was found guilty of fifty two of the fifty three murders and sentenced to death for each offense. On the 14 February 1994, he was executed with a single gunshot behind the right ear in the soundproofed execution room in Novocherkassk prison.

27 AMY GILLIGAN (AMERICAN) 5-50

Sister Amy Duggan Archer-Gilligan was a Connecticut nursing home proprietor and serial killer who was the inspiration for the film *Arsenic and Old Lace*. Her confirmed kill is five but the true number is closer to fifty.

Amy was born in Milton, Connecticut in October 1868 to James Duggan and Mary Kennedy. She was the eighth of ten children. She was educated at the local school and later at New Britain Normal School. In 1907 Amy and her husband, James Archer, moved to Windsor where they set up their own business, the *Archer Home for the Elderly and Infirm*. She was regarded as a pioneer in health care in Connecticut offering enticements "for elderly people and chronic invalids," who could benefit from lifetime care simply by signing over their life insurance policies or donating $1,000, on check in. In 1910 Amy's husband died suddenly from diseased kidneys or Bright's disease. Three years later she married wealthy Michael W. Gilligan who also died a year later. Although the business continued to thrive locals could not help noticing that between 1907 and 1917 sixty of the elderly residents passed away. Twelve died between 1907 and 1910, but forty eight died between 1911 and 1916. She was eventually charged with five counts of murder following a fraud investigation on one of her deceased residents. However, her lawyers managed to get the charges reduced to a single count of murder, that of Franklin R. Andrews. On the 18 June 1917 she was found guilty and sentenced to death. But the verdict was eventually reversed on a technicality and during a second trial she pleaded guilty to second-degree murder and received life imprisonment. In 1924 she was declared insane and transferred to the state mental hospital in Middletown. She remained there until her death in 1962 by which time she had survived nearly everyone connected with the case.

28 ROBERT W. PICKTON (CANADIAN) 49+

Robert William Pickton is Canada's most prolific rapist and serial killer who slaughtered 49, mostly drug addicted, sex workers and fed them to the pigs on his farm. He was convicted of six murders. His first criminal trial took over a year. His trial and conviction has so far cost the Canadian state almost $80,000,000.

Willie Pickton was born on the 24 October 1949 in Port Coquitlam in British Columbia in Canada. His parents were Leonard and Helen Louise Pickton and he has one brother called Dave and a sister called Linda. His parents were pig farmers from a long line of pig farmers. In 1963 they bought forty acres of swamp land for $18,000 at 953 Dominion Avenue later to become Vancouver's Ground Zero. By 1994 the land was worth $7,200,000. Some of it was sold, and some retained as a pig farm.

Around about the same time women began to go missing at an alarming rate from the DES (Vancouver's Downtown Eastside). Willie's brother Dave opened up a dive called *Piggy's Palace* which soon became the place for boozers, bikers, hookers, ex-cons, druggies, orgies and pig roasted on the spit supplied by their hog farm from pigs fed on humans. Pickton's *modus operandi* was to pick up prostitutes bring them back to the farm and then rape, torture and butcher them before feeding their mutilated bodies to the pigs. It took a long time to eventually catch him due to the indifference and incompetence of both the RCMP and the Vancouver Police Department. Pickton was eventually convicted of six second degree murders and sentenced on the 11 December 2007 to 25 years in prison without the possibility of parole. In sentencing him the Judge added: "Mr. Pickton's conduct was murderous and repeatedly so. I cannot know the details but I know this: What happened to them was senseless and despicable."

29 MANUEL VILLEGAS (SPANISH) 7-48

Manuel Delgado Villegas aka *El Arropiero* was a Spanish serial killer who claimed to have committed a total of 48 killings in Spain, Italy and France between 1964 and 1971. He was never convicted of any of these killings as he was deemed insane and sent to a mental institution. Manuel was born on the 25 January 1943 in Seville, Spain to José Delgado Martín and his wife. His mother died aged 24 while giving birth to him. He had one sibling, a sister called Joaquina. Because of the nature of his father's job, he was a travelling salesman, Manuel and his sister were sent to live with their grandmother in Andalucía. Although he attended school he failed to read and write.

At 18 he enlisted in the Spanish Legion where he was trained how to kill a victim by his hand. It was later to be part of his *modus operandi*. After leaving the Legion he became a vagrant, and began his indiscriminate campaign of killing in 1964 when he killed a chef who was sunbathing on the beach. His *modus operandi* showed he was not an organized killer, nothing was ever premeditated. He would kill on a whim and often did. He would become enraged by a simple comment and this would cause him to act in a violent and brutal manner. He would kill by battering his victim with a blunt instrument or his bare hands by beating with his fists or strangling with his hands. He attacked to rob and or rape but would only rape his victim after he had killed them. He had no particular victim preference and was known to kill old and young, rich and poor, homosexual and heterosexual, foreign and local, and men and women which made it difficult for law enforcement agencies to link his killings. His total confirmed kill was seven people. But there were many others killed so the total remains unconfirmed. After his confession he was interned in a mental institution. He died there from a smoking related lung disease.

30 GERALD E. STANO (AMERICAN) 0-41

Gerald Eugene Stano was a little known American offender who was considered to be a serial killer. He claimed to have murdered 41 women in Florida, Pennsylvania and New Jersey between 1971 and 1998. But many commentators believe he was more of a serial confessor rather than a serial killer. His case is surrounded by controversy. One detective, Paul Crow, was later removed from office for corruption in "spoon-feeding" lists of murders to Stano in order to get him to confess to them. Furthermore, Stano was only ever convicted of one murder, that of seventeen year old Cathy Lee Scharf, and there is now serious doubt of his guilt.

Gerald Stano was born Paul Zeininger on the 12 September 1951 in Schenectady, New York. After six months he was adopted by Eugene and Norma Stano, a manager and nurse, who renamed him Gerald Eugene Stano. Although given the opportunity of a loving family Gerald exhibited discipline problems from day one. As a child he suffered from severe enuresis. An average student, except for music at which he excelled, Gerald was a pathological liar and petty thief.

Initially, he drifted from job to job and was fired from some for stealing. His life turned for the better in 1975 when he married a 22 year old hairdresser; but it didn't last. When arrested on an assault charge he suddenly began confessing to murders. Prosecutors then agreed that if he pleaded guilty to three murders other murders would be taken into account. He received three life sentences on the 2 September, 1981. He then confessed to other murders for which he was sentenced to death. Realizing his mistake he appealed but all appeals were rejected and he was eventually executed on the 23 March 1998 in Florida State Prison. But what he innocent of all charges?

31 BELLE GUNNESS (NORWAY-USA) 40+

America's most successful Black Widow fraudster and serial killer who poisoned over forty people, boys and girls, men and women was born Brynhild Paulsdatter Størset on the 11 November 1859 in Norway. Her parents were dirt poor farmers. She emigrated to America in 1881 and changed her name to Belle Gunness. She settled in Chicago where she met and married her first husband Mads Sorenson. They were blessed with five children. He died in 1900 from heart failure and Belle collected on two life policies. She then married Peter Gunness and they ran a successful farm together in La Porte, Indiana. He died unexpectedly but luckily he was also heavily insured. She continued to run the farm herself up until 1907 when she employed Ray Lamphere, initially as a farm hand. They soon became lovers. Around this time Belle began an advertising campaign seeking a suitable husband. Many were called, some were chosen, few left. Belle fleeced them of their wealth and they all "disappeared".

When the farmhouse burned down leaving her and her children's charred remains Ray Lamphere was charged with their murder. But was the headless corpse that of Belle Gunness? Now investigators had an even bigger problem. As the dig at the farm continued more and more bodies were being uncovered. At Lamphere's trial he tried to prove that the body found was not that of Belle Gunness but someone else. He was acquitted of murder, found guilty of arson and sentenced to 25 years imprisonment. On the 30 December 1909 he died from tuberculosis. Prior to his death he admitted that the fire and fake death of Gunness had been planned by them both but she had double-crossed him and fled with the fortune she had stolen from her 42 potential suitors, a fortune which today would amount to over $6,000,000. She lived the life of a Duchess thereafter.

32 PATRICK KEARNEY (AMERICAN) 28-40

Patrick Kearney aka the *Freeway Killer* is a homosexual necrophiliac and brutal psychopathic pedophile and serial killer who, together with David Hill, murdered between 8-40 boys and young men in California between 1962 and 1977. Their campaign ended at 1:30 p.m. on Friday the 1 July 1977 when they walked into the reception area of the Riverside County Sherriff's Office, pointed to a Wanted Poster, and told the stunned deputy: "We're them." It was finally the end of a murder campaign that spanned fifteen years.

Patrick Wayne Kearney was born on the 24 September 1949 in East Los Angeles to George and Eunice Kearney. He had a miserable childhood and was bullied at school and called a "faggot." In 1957 he graduated High School and shortly afterwards he himself moved to Long Beach, California. In 1958, at the age of nineteen, he joined the U.S. Air Force and after he was discharged, hooked up with a waster called David Hill. They became on and off lovers. It was during one of these off times, in the spring of 1962, that Kearney began his killing campaign. Why he needed to rape, torture and kill we will never know. He lived in a nice apartment in Golden Avenue in Long Beach. He had a good job as a aeronautics engineer earning a colossal $20,000 a year as a Senior Research Assistant at Hughes Aircraft in Culver city. He killed in America and also in Mexico and rarely deviated from his *modus operandi* which involved abducting, shooting, sodomizing, mutilating and dumping the bodies of young boys and men he picked up. By 1974 he was killing victims at the rate of one a month. He eventually surrendered and confessed to 28 murders later increased to 35. He was charged with 21 and pleaded guilty. The judge called him an "an insult to humanity." As of June 2014 Kearney is incarcerated in the California State Prison, Mule Creek.

33 KASPARS PETROVS (LATVIAN) 13-38

Outside Latvia, few people ever heard of Kaspars Petrovs aka *Würger von Riga* (the Riga Strangler) but Petrovs is the most prolific and notorious serial killer in Latvian history. He is responsible for the deaths of at least 38 elderly women between 2000 and 2003 in Riga although he was only officially convicted of 13 murders.

He was born in Grobiņa, Latvia in 1978 the son of two prominent medical doctors. In his teenage years he ran away from home and drifted from place to place. He had no fixed abode and slept wherever he could. For some unknown reason, Kaspars had a fixation on elderly women. When arrested for robbery he confessed to killing in excess of 30 elderly women. He was initially charged with 38 murders, 8 attempted murders and various thefts and robberies but the murder counts were later reduced to 13 due to insufficient evidence. He was tried in 2005 and said that he did not intend to kill his elderly victims but merely wanted to rob them. His *modus operandi* was either to force his way into the homes of single elderly women sometimes posing as an official of the state gas company, *Latvijas gaze*. Sometimes he would befriend them at the post office or offer to carry home their shopping. He would kill the occupant usually by strangling them with a towel and then place them on the bed as if they were sleeping. He would then search the home for cash and valuables. When he left he would lock the door. Many of the victims were not found for days. Some were still breathing when he left them. His crimes netted him over a quarter of a million euro. It was by pure accident that he was eventually arrested. Forensics found fingerprints in one of the apartments of a victim. These were compared with the central file. He was arrested on the 3 February 2003. After his conviction in the Riga Regional Court on the 12 May 2005 he asked for forgiveness.

34 WILLIAM G. BONIN (AMERICAN) 14-36

American serial killer and sexual degenerate William George Bonin aka the *Freeway Killer* raped, sodomized, tortured and murdered between 21 and 36 boys and young men between 1979 and 1980 in California. He was convicted of 14 murders and executed on the 23 February 1996 in San Quentin State Prison by lethal injection.

William was born on the 8 January 1947 in Connecticut in January 1947. He was the middle son of alcoholic parents who were unwilling and unable to take care of him. He spent most of his early childhood in state institutions where he was continuously molested. He joined the US army and saw service in Vietnam. Afterwards he moved to California. Between 1968 and 1971 he was involved in several sexual assaults on young men and was sent to prison and ordered to undergo medical treatment. He was released in May 1974 after doctors certified that he was "no longer a danger to others." Big mistake. He, with others, began a brutal campaign which involved the abduction, rape, torture and murder of up to 36 young men. Bonin had a particular *modus operandi*. His victims were usually aged between 12-19 and ranged from schoolboys to hitchhikers to male prostitutes. He would entice or force them into the back of his Chevrolet camper van, tie them up and kill them. He preferred to strangle them with their own clothes although sometimes he would stab or batter them to death. But first, he would take his time to torture and sexually abuse them. He later dumped their bodies along various freeways in California. He was convicted of a total of 14 murders committed between August 1979 and June 1980. While in custody Bonin actually confessed to abducting, raping, and killing 21 boys and young men with the assistance of Vernon Butts. Bonin spent a total of fourteen years on Death Row before finally being executed on the 23 February 1996 by lethal injection.

35 JOHN WAYNE GACY (AMERICAN) 35+

John Wayne Gacy, one of America's most prolific serial killers, was named after an all American hero. At one stage in his life he was a successful businessman, happily married with two loving children. But he went on to rape, torture and kill thirty five young men most of whom he buried in the crawl space underneath his house. He was known as *Pogo the Clown* and the *Killer Clown*.

John Wayne Jr. was born on the 17 March 1942 in Chicago, Illinois. He was the second of three children born to John Wayne Gacy and Marion Elaine Robinson. The family lived in a middle class area. He had a difficult relationship with his father who was a tyrant, a bully and an alcoholic. But by 1967 life couldn't have been better for John Gacy. He was happily married with two children and had a job running three KFC franchises for his father in law. Then disaster struck. On the 10 May 1968 he was indicted on sodomy charges. He later pleaded guilty and was given an unexpected ten year sentence. His life fell apart and his wife left him. But he became a model prisoner and was paroled after 18 months. He worked his way back up and formed his own construction and renovation company PDM and remarried. His new wife was a friend of Gacy's younger sister. She was aware of his time in prison but believed he had changed. She moved into his home with her two children soon after the couple announced their engagement. But all of this just afforded him the opportunity to continue to abuse young boys; except it got much worse. His wife left him and he began picking up young men, bringing them home, torturing and raping them and then killing them before burying them in the crawl space under his house. He was eventually caught, tried and confessed that since 1972 he had killed 25-30 times. Convicted of 33 murders his final words before his execution on the 10 May 1994 were "Kiss my ass."

36 ADOLFO CONSTANZO (AMERICAN) 30

Twenty six year old Adolfo de Jesús Constanzo known as *El Padrino de Matamoros*, died on the 6 May 1989 after he instructed one of his cohorts, Alvaro de Leon, to shoot him dead in their apartment in Mexico city so as to avoid capture by Mexican authorities. Constanzo was a cult leader, drug dealer and American serial killer responsible for the deaths of at least 30 men, women and children.

Adolfo was born on the 1 November 1962 in Miami, Florida to Della Aurora Gonzalez del Valle, a fifteen year old Cuban immigrant. When he was just six months old his mother had him blessed by a Haitian high priest who practiced *palo mayombe*. When he was a teenager he was apprenticed to a local sorcerer. By the time he was twenty one Constanzo converted to *Kadiempembe*, his religion's version of Satan.

He left Miami for Mexico city where he recruited his first disciples: Martin Quintana Rodriguez and Omar Orea Ochoa. Constanzo seduced both of them alternating them as his "man" and his "woman." He then began making premonitions for local drug cartels to ensure their shipments were not detected. Word spread of his "magical" powers and he became friendly with many of the drug lords. Eventually he moved into the drug business himself and began eliminating his enemies and anyone else he didn't like. By 1986 he had 30 powerful and devoted followers and had also amassed a considerable fortune. Around this time he began substituting animals for humans in his voodoo-type sacrifices. The authorities believe he murdered 23 people in human sacrifices in Mexico city alone. But it was his sacrificial murder of American medical student, Mark Kilroy, that sealed his fate. He fled to Mexico City with four of his followers and on the 6 May 1989 he died during a shoot-out with police.

37 DEAN A. CORLL (AMERICAN) 6-28

Dean Corll was known by locals as the *Candy Man* but he wasn't a sweet natured young boy. Corll was an American serial killer who, with two accomplices, David Brooks and Elmer Wayne, abducted, raped, tortured, and murdered a minimum of 28 boys in a series of killings spanning from 1970 to 1973 in Houston, Texas. The killings were later referred to as the *Houston Mass Murders*. At the time of their discovery, they were considered the worst example of serial murder in American history.

Corll was born on the 24 December 1939 in Fort Wayne, Indiana, the first child of Mary Robinson and Arnold Edwin Corll. He had an unhappy childhood. His father, a strict disciplinarian, was constantly bickering with his mother and they divorced in 1946 and re-married four years later before divorcing again in 1953. He was drafted into the United States Army in 1964 and discharged in 1965, after ten months of service. It was in this period that he first realized he was homosexual. He then returned to Houston. He first met 12 year old Brooks in 1967. Later on he was to pay Brooks $200 for ever victim he lured to Corll's home. Between 1970-1973, Corll killed 28 young men aged between 13-20. Most were abducted from Houston Heights with the assistance of either Brooks or Henley. The *modus operandi* was that once they were in Corll's home, they were plied with alcohol or drugs. They were either tied to his bed or a plywood torture board and raped, tortured and beaten, sometimes for days. After this, they were either strangled or shot, wrapped in plastic and dumped. During one of these torture session on the 8 August 1973 Henley shot Corll in the head following an argument. He called the police and confessed to the murders telling them that sometimes Corll castrated the victims while still alive. Police later discovered several severed genitals in his home in sealed plastic bags.

38 JUAN VALLEJO CORONA (MEXICAN) 25+

Juan Vallejo Corona, the *Machete Murderer*, is a Mexican serial killer responsible for a minimum of 25 killings in California during 1971 making it, at the time, the worst and most notorious confirmed serial killings in American history. Corona was born in Autlán, Jalisco state, Mexico in 1934. He first entered the USA at 16 illegally crossing the Mexican border into California to pick fruit in the Imperial Valley. Later, he moved to the Marysville-Yuba City area in May 1953, and worked as a laborer on a local ranch. He was so deeply affected by the death and destruction that was caused in December 1955 when a major flood devastated Northern California killing 38 people, that he suffered a mental breakdown.

In 1962, he became a licensed labor contractor and was hiring workers to staff the local fruit ranches. He chose a workforce made up of drifters, down-and-outs, alcoholics, and the elderly. They worked hard every day for below minimum wages and slept in dismal lodgings on the Sullivan ranch. Corona had total control over their needs and food and in 1971 he decided to abuse that control to satisfy his own personal sadistic sexual needs. In 1971, during a period of six weeks, Corona who was married, began a systematic campaign of rape, torture and murder on his men. His *modus operandi* was simple and unsophisticated. After choosing a victim, he dug a shallow grave for them. He then raped them and stabbed them to death before hacking off their heads with a machete and throwing them in the shallow grave. He was tried and on the 23 September 1982 convicted on 25 counts of murder. He is currently serving his sentence at Corcoran State Prison, in California. Denied parole on the 5 December 2011, he can re-apply in 2016. According to the New York Daily News in June 2014 he is now almost totally blind and demented.

39 DAGMAR OVERBYE (DANISH) 9-25

Dagmar Johanne Amalie Overbye was a serial child murderer and Denmark's most notorious serial killer. Between 1913 and 1920 she murdered between 9-25 infant children. She was sentenced to death on the 3 March 1921. Her sentence was later commuted to life imprisonment. Her case was responsible for the introduction of the first proper child care provisions in Denmark for children born out of wedlock.

Dagmar was born on the 23 April 1887 in the small village Assendrup near Aarhus. Her parents, Sean and Anne Marie Overbye, were poor farmers. Dagmar was a moody and melancholic child. She worked as a servant girl with various families. In 1912 she married Jens Sorensen Fine but it was an unhappy relationship and she left him and went, with her daughter Erena, to live in Copenhagen. After the failure of a sweet shop business she began working as a professional child caretaker. She specialized in caring for children born out of wedlock and set up an unofficial adoption agency. Dagmar would take the infants in, promise to look after them until such time as she was able to place them with good decent families, accept the payment from the mostly impoverished mother and then either strangle, drown or burn the infant in her masonry heater. It was by pure chance that her gruesome crimes were discovered. She was reported to the police by Karoline Aagesen who had placed her child in Dagmar's care and then changed her mind. She went to the police and told them her story. Overbye was arrested and confessed to the deaths of 16 children. She was charged with 9 murders but suspected of at least 25. Overbye was tried, convicted and sentenced to death. The reigning monarch Christian X commuted the sentence to one of life imprisonment. Overbye died in the Western Prison on the 6 May 1929 at the age of forty two.

40 CARL PANZRAM (AMERICAN) 22+

Some say that Carl Panzram was the most vicious, evil, depraved serial rapist and killer that America has ever known. He hated everyone including himself. He tortured, raped and murdered in America, South America, Africa and Europe. He admitted to killing at least 22 people and raping 1,000 boys and men, just because he could. He wrote his own biography and never ever expressed remorse for any heinous act he ever committed. He was finally hanged at Leavenworth Federal Penitentiary in 1930. He was certainly a fascinating evil degenerate.

He was born on the 28 June 1891 in East Grand Forks, in rural Minnesota, America. His parents, John (Johann) and Lizzie, were poor Prussian immigrants who worked an almost destitute farm. He was institutionalized as a child and severely abused which bred in him a hatred of mankind. At 19 he had no home, no job, no skills, no family or loved ones, no hope and no future. All he had was a burning desire to seek revenge for the brutality he had suffered inside and outside of state institutions. He began his campaign of terror drifting across Kansas, Texas and up into California, all the way robbing, thieving, burning and raping, without mercy. He drifted from town to town, using different aliases. He just wanted boys and men, not to love, but to rape.

Panzram graduated to serial killing in 1920. His *modus operandi* was to lure sailors in New York away from bars, get them drunk, rape them and shoot them with a Colt .45 pistol. Later he dumped their bodies near Execution Rocks Light in Long Island Sound. He killed ten sailors in this way before sailing up to Luanda in Angola. Here he claimed to have raped a number of boys and killed two of them. He was arrested in July 1928, confessed and was sentenced to death and hanged on the 5 September, 1930.

41 MARY ANN COTTON (BRITISH) 21+

Little known Mary Ann Cotton was an English poisoner who was convicted of murdering her children and up to 21 people altogether, mainly by arsenic poisoning. Many scholars regard her as Britain's first serial killer.

She was born Mary Ann Robson on the 31 October 1832 at Low Moorsley, Sunderland in England. In 1852, she married William Mowbray. They were blessed with five children, but cursed when four died from gastric fever. They then lost three more children. Her husband died of an intestinal disorder in January 1865 and Mary collected on his life insurance. After her husband's death she moved to Seaham where her three year old daughter died. She now had just one child left out of nine. She married George Ward on the 28 August 1865 and he died a year later after a long illness. Luckily for her he was covered by substantial life insurance. In 1867 she married James Robinson, and a short time later their child died. He became suspicious and threw her out. Desperate and living rough, she was introduced to widower Frederick Cotton by his sister, her friend Margaret. She moved in and soon became pregnant with her eleventh child. That December Frederick Cotton died from a stomach ailment. Once again Mary collected the insurance money. Other lovers came and died and eventually the press began an investigation. They discovered that she had moved around a lot and had lost three husbands, a lover, her mother and a dozen children to stomach ailments. Cotton was arrested and tried in 1873. After deliberating for just ninety minutes the jury found her guilty of murder. She was hanged at Durham County jail on 24 March 1873 by Mr. William Calcraft who completely botched the job. Because the drop below the trap door was too short, Mary was left dangling on the end of the rope until the executioner pressed down upon her long enough to ensure her death.

42 THIERRY PAULIN (FRENCH) 21

Thierry Paulin aka the *Monster of Montmartre* was a minor celebrity French serial killer who murdered 21 victims between 1984 and1987. He was born on the 28 November 1963 in *Fort-de-France*, Martinique. His father, Gaby, abandoned him and his seventeen year old mother, Rose Helena Larcher, soon after he was born. At eighteen months, his mother passed him over to his paternal grandmother and he stayed in her beachside restaurant in the resort of *L'Anse-à-Ane* until the age of ten.

He briefly joined the navy and was assigned to the Naval Air Station, *Toussus-le-Noble*, in the Yvelines. Around 1985 he became a waiter and part-time drag artist singing Eartha Kitt songs at the *Paradis Latin*, a night-club in the Latin Quarter, renowned for its transvestite shows. It was here that he met and fell in love with nineteen year old drug addict and dealer Jean-Thierry Mathurin who was originally from French Guyana. They moved in together and quickly became prominent members of the Paris gay community; attending all the fashionable parties and being treated like minor celebrities. They financed their lifestyle by robbing and brutally killing elderly women. The killings became front page news. They stopped for a while. But Paulin couldn't stop forever. Between Christmas 1985 and the middle of June 1986 eight more elderly women were robbed and murdered. Police were now convinced that the murders were linked to the 1984 murders due to fingerprint evidence. But the *modus operandi* of the 1986 killer was slightly different. The killer didn't spend as much time beating the women. Aware he had HIV, Paulin began a lavish lifestyle using the proceeds of his crimes to fund it. Eventually captured he admitted to a total of 21 murders. He was sent to prison to await his trial but in early 1988 he became seriously ill as a result of the AIDS virus and died in April 1989 in the hospital wing of Fresnes prison.

43 MARTHA BECK (AMERICAN) 20+

Martha Beck together with her lover Raymond Fernandez (qv) were the notorious *Lonely Hearts Killers* who are believed to have robbed and murdered as many as 20 lonely hearts women in America in the 1940s. However, they were only ever convicted of a single murder.

Martha was born Martha Seabrook on the 6 May 1920 in Milton, Florida. She suffered from a glandular condition that caused her be an obese lady all her life. She also suffered from low self-esteem and depression. She qualified as a nurse and was excellent at her job. She married once and had two children but the marriage was a disaster and ended soon after. She was desperate to meet someone, anyone, and decided to join a lonely hearts club. She received her first and only reply on Christmas Eve 1947 from Raymond Fernandez, a liar, a cheat and an all-round conman who seduced women and left them penniless. She became so infatuated with him that she decided to team up with him. Together they scammed vulnerable woman all over America but now they also began killing them. They were finally arrested on the 28 February 1949 and brought back to the District Attorney's office in Kent County where their interrogation began. On the basis they would be tried there, they both confessed. But the DA reneged on the deal and they were then transferred to New York, a state with the death penalty, in relation to the murder of Janet Fay. They were assigned a single lawyer between the two of them which was a clear breach of their constitutional rights. It was a sensational trial with bizarre tales of sex, deception and murder. It made headline news for months. They were tried and convicted for the murder of Janet Fay who they had killed in Albany, New York. They were sentenced to death and executed in the electric chair on the 8 March 1951 in Sing Sing.

44 RAY FERNANDEZ (AMERICAN) 20+

Raymond Fernandez together with his lover Martha Beck (qv) were the notorious *Lonely Hearts Killers* who are believed to have murdered as many as 20 women in the 1940s. Raymond Martinez Fernandez was born in Hawaii of Spanish parents on the 17 December 1914. In 1932, Raymond decided to visit his uncle in Spain and work on his farm. At 20 he met and married a local girl called Encarnacion Robles and they set up home.

With the onset of World War II Raymond joined the Spanish merchant navy but was soon recruited by the British Secret Service and worked for them as a spy. Afterwards he moved to America and began seducing lonely women and fleecing them of their savings. He had no work so he passed the time by writing letters to "lonely hearts" clubs searching for vulnerable, gullible and lonely women. His *modus operandi* was simple. He would dispatch dozens of letters every week to different women, gain their trust, seduce them and then rob them blind before disappearing forever. Most of the women were too embarrassed to report the incidents to the police. Sometimes, they suspected they were being conned but hoped that Raymond would eventually fall in love with them and change. He later hooked up with Martha Beck and the murder campaign became prolific. They were eventually caught and in 1949 tried in New York for the murder of Janet Fay. Fernandez, although he had previously confessed to her murder, now decided to plead not guilty. He now said he had made admissions to the Michigan authorities but these were simply to protect Martha, the woman he loved. After a trial lasting 44 days they were both convicted and sentenced to death. It was the only murder for which they were tried although they were suspects in twenty other cases. They were executed by electric chair on the 10 October 1949.

45 LAWRENCE BITTAKER (AMERICAN) 5-19

Lawrence Sigmund Bittaker is a rapist and serial killer who together with Roy Lewis Norris were known as the *Tool Box Killers*. In 1979 the pair kidnapped, raped, brutally tortured and killed five teenage girls in southern California. He is currently on death row in San Quentin State Prison awaiting execution. Despite numerous opportunities to do so, he has never expressed any regret for the suffering he inflicted upon his victims. FBI Agent, John Douglas, once described him as the most disturbing individual he ever profiled.

Lawrence didn't have much of a chance in life growing up. He was born Lawrence Sigmund on the 27 September 1940 in Pittsburgh, Pennsylvania. His biological parents put him up for adoption and he was placed in an orphanage before being adopted by George Bittaker and his wife. Despite an IQ of 138 he never did well at school and was more interested in petty larceny. His criminal career began when he was just twelve and lasted all his life. In fact, Bittaker spent more time in prison than out of it. In 1974 he hooked up with fellow convict Roy Norris. The pair struck up a friendship, a partnership from Hell. Their *modus operandi* was to abduct young women or lure them into their 1977 GMC silver cargo van with no side windows and a large passenger sliding door which they equipped with clothes, a cooler filled with beer, restraints, a mattress and a tool box packed with torture instruments. They would then bring them up the mountains where they would sexually tortured their victims before killing them. When caught each blamed the other and eventually Norris agreed to testify against Bittaker who in 1971 was found guilty and sentenced to death for the five counts of first degree murder. Bittaker awaits execution on San Quentin's Death Row. Always the coward, he has spent the rest of his life trying to prevent his execution.

46 JOHN N. COLLINS (CANADIAN) 1-18

John Collins, who was known as the *Co-Ed Killer*, is a sadistic Canadian serial sex killer responsible for the *Michigan Murders*, a series of highly publicized killings in the Ann Arbor-Ypsilanti area of Michigan between 1967 and 1969.

Collins was born on the 17 June 1947 in Windsor, Ontario in Canada. He was the youngest child of Richard and Loretta Chapman. After his parents divorced his mother remarried but the marriage broke down after just a year. She then re-located to America and settled in Detroit where she married and later divorced William Collins. By nine he had seen three fathers come and go, each one worse than the other. Growing up Collins was a curious mixture of a sex obsessed teenager with a puritanical streak. Although he seemed like a perfectly, well-adjusted young man with good manners and respect for authority he was a sadistic psychopath. His campaign of terror lasted between 1967 and 1969 and in that period he is believed to have raped, tortured and murdered at least six women.

When he was arrested he vehemently denied having any involvement in any killings. But police weren't convinced. His name kept cropping up. It was too much of a coincidence. When police conducted their own background investigations on their suspect they discovered that he had an extensive history of sexual harassment and violence against women; was obsessed with mutilation and excessive gore and had, several years previously, badly beaten up his sister's boyfriend causing him to be hospitalized. Because of the lack of evidence in seven other killings, Collins was only charged with one murder, that of Karen Beineman. His trial began in August 1970 and he was found guilty and imprisoned for life with no parole. He later changed his name to Chapman.

47 JOEL DAVID RIFKIN (AMERICAN) 9-18

American serial killer Joel David Rifkin aka *Joel the Ripper* was convicted of the murder of nine women working as prostitutes in the New York area between 1989 and 1993 However, he is believed to have been responsible for seventeen or eighteen deaths.

He was born on the 20 January 1959. His natural born mother and biological father were both college students who put him up for adoption as soon as he was born. Benjamin Rifkin and his wife Jeanne nee Granelles were pleased to adopt him. The Rifkins moved to the East Meadows district of New York when Joel was six and he enjoyed a normal loving upbringing. Although he joined the Cub Scouts he was shy and insular and easily bullied at school. After graduating from East Meadows High School Joel became obsessed with escorts. Two years after his father died Rifkin committed his first murder. Her body has never been found. He picked up the young woman in the East Village near the East River and brought her back to his home in East Meadows which he shared with his sister and elderly mother. He had sex with her, killed her and then mutilated her body. In the following four years Rifkin killed another sixteen women. His *modus operandi* was the same. Many were drug addicts and almost all were young women working as prostitutes. He picked them up in Manhattan and either had sex with them in his car or brought them back to his home. He then strangled them to death, mutilated their bodies and dumped the body parts in different places. Rifkin soon became the most prolific serial killer in the history of New York City. It was only by pure chance that he was caught. After his arrest he confessed and was convicted in 1994 of nine counts of second degree murder and sentenced to 203 years to life in prison. Some believe Rifkin is also responsible for some of the *Long Island Prostitute Murders* which he denies.

48 JEFFREY DAHMER (AMERICAN) 17

Known as the *Milwaukee Cannibal*, Jeffrey Dahmer, rapist, cannibal, necrophile and serial killer is among the best known of all American serial killers. He was convicted of seventeen murders between 1978 and 1981 and was himself murdered by a fellow inmate in prison.

He was born on the 21 May, 1960 in West Allis, Wisconsin, to Joyce and Lionel Herbert Dahmer. He was their first born. Dahmer's father Lionel, was a Chemistry student at Marquette University. His mother Joyce was employed as a teletype machine instructor. Initially, it was a loving household and as a toddler Jeffrey wanted for nothing. He was enrolled in Revere High School and right from the get go, was considered odd. His parents separated in 1978 and this had a detrimental effect on Jeffrey. He began to drink heavily. He drifted and then later moved in with his grandmother. In January 1985 he eventually got a job as a mixer at the Milwaukee Ambrosia Chocolate Factory and began to check out the Milwaukee gay scene and frequent its gay bars, bookstores and bathhouses. After a period of nine years he began to kill again. He would lure young men back to his house for sex, kill them, mutilate them, eat parts of them, and retain their body parts to use as a stimulus for masturbation. He was arrested after police accidentally found incriminating photographs in his apartment of dead men. They also found, *inter alia*, four severed heads, seven skulls, in the fridge the freshly severed head of a black male; two human hearts, an arm muscle, and an entire torso on his freezer. The chief medical officer was later to comment: "It was more like dismantling someone's museum than an actual crime scene." He confessed to all his crimes and was convicted of a total of sixteen murders and sentenced to life. On the 28 November 1994 he was beaten to death by a fellow prisoner.

49 DONATO BILANCIA (ITALIAN) 17)

Donato Walter Bilancia, known as the *Monster of Liguria*, is Italy's most notorious serial killer. He was responsible for seventeen murders on the Italian Riviera between 1997 and 1998. He was born Donato Bilancia on the 10 July 1951 in a small village near Potenza in southern Italy. His abusive father worked as a clerk and his mother was a housewife. At the age of five, his family moved to Piedmont and then Genoa in the Liguria region in northern Italy.

He dropped out of high school and drifted through several jobs but it was robbing he liked best. A loner, he was a regular visitor to Genoa's *Foce*, the red light district. But, he had no record of violence until 1997 when he was betrayed by his best friend, his accomplice and wife all of whom he murdered. These were revenge killings but the motive for the next three was financial gain. He killed a jeweler, his wife and a money changer. He then began to murder at random, killing because he couldn't stop. His next victims included three night watchmen, an Albanian prostitute, a Ukrainian prostitute, a Russian prostitute, a money changer, a Nigerian prostitute, and two random women he encountered on a train. He was identified by a victim who escaped death. He was finally arrested and charged. Rejecting a plea of diminished responsibility, court appointed experts testified that Bilancia fully understood the morality and consequences of his actions. Following an eleven month trial and having deliberated for five hours the court sentenced him to thirteen terms of life imprisonment plus twenty years. He did not attend court and watched the proceedings on CCTV in his cell at Chiavari prison. The judge recommended that he never be released from prison. He lost two appeals and is currently serving his sentence in a Padua prison where he is kept under constant suicide watch.

50 DENNIS NILSEN (BRITISH) 15-16

Dennis Nilsen aka the *Kindly Killer* is one of Britain's most notorious necrophiliacs and serial killers. He was born in Stricken, Fraserburg near Scotland's windswept north-eastern on the 23 November 1945 and enjoyed a happy childhood.

In later life he joined the catering corps of the Royal Fusiliers, City of London Regiment of the British Army when he was just sixteen. While in the Middle East Dennis realized he was homosexual. He left the army in 1972 and joined the Metropolitan Police but left the police after just a year due the homophobic and macho atmosphere that prevailed in the force. Thereafter he worked as a civil servant in a Jobcentre. A homosexual who killed because he was lonely and wanted to live with the corpses of the victims he killed, Dennis was known to put them under the floorboards, take them out, wash them, clothe them, sit them in front of the television and later have sex with them. He was caught when the body parts he had mutilated and flushed down the toilet were uncovered by a drainage expert when the plumbing system clogged up.

Steven Sinclair was his fifteenth and final victim. While on bail for theft he met Dennis in Oxford Street on the 26 January 1983. He went back to Nilsen's flat and while sitting listening to music Nilsen strangled him with a tie attached to a piece of string. Then there was the usual routine. Dennis bathed him and put him into the bed. Afterwards he dismembered his body. He decapitated his head and left it to boil in a pot while he took his dog Bleep for his customary walk. Later he tried to flush part of him down the drain. When Dyno Rod discovered the blockage to the drains was caused by human bones Nilsen was arrested. He made a full and frank confession. He was found guilty of 15 murders and sentenced to life in prison.

CHAPTER SIX
BIBLIOGRAPHY

Dietz, M.L. (1986), Killing Sequentially: Expanding the Parameters of the Conceptualisation of Serial and Mass Killers". In T.O'Reilley-Flemming, (Ed.), Serial and Mass Murder: Theory Research and Policy. Toronto: Canadian Scholars Press

Dietz PE, Hazelwood RR & Warren J 1990. The sexually sadistic criminal and his offenses. Bulletin of the American Academy of Psychiatry and the Law 18(2): 163–178

Egger, S.A. (1984) A Working Definition of Serial Murder and the Reduction of Linkage Blindness, Journal of Police Science and Administration, 12: 348-357

Egger, S.A. (1997). The Killers Among Us: An Examination of Serial Murder and its Investigation. Upper Saddle River, NJ: Prentice Hall.

Folino JO (2000) Sexual homicides and their classification according to motivation: a report from Argentina. International Journal of Offender Therapy and Comparative Criminology 44(6): 740–750

Fox, James Alan; Jack Levin (2005), Extreme Killing: Understanding Serial and Mass Murder, Sage

Holmes RM & De Burger JE (1998), Profiles in terror: the serial murderer, in Holmes RM & Holmes ST (eds), Contemporary perspectives on serial murder. Thousand Oaks: Sage: 5–16

Holmes, Ronald M.; Stephen T. Holmes (1998), Contemporary Perspectives on Serial Murder, SAGE Kraemer GW, Lord WD & Heilbrun K 2004. Comparing single and serial homicide offenses. Behavioral sciences and the law 22(3): 325–343

Morton, R.J. (2005) Serial murder multi-disciplinary perspectives for investigation. FBI

Mouzos J & West D (2007), An examination of serial murder in Australia. Trends and issues in crime and criminal justice no. 346.

ABOUT THE AUTHOR

David Elio Malocco was born in Dundalk, County Louth, Ireland. His father was born in Casalattico in Frosinone in Italy and his mother was born in Monaghan in Ireland. He was educated at the Christian Brothers School in Dundalk and his parents later sent him to St. Patricks College in Cavan where they hoped he would be ordained as a Catholic priest. But he chose law and business instead.

He received his Bachelor of Civil Law degree from University College Dublin and spent fifteen years as a criminal lawyer before taking a second degree at the Open University, Milton Keynes in England where he obtained a first class honors degree in Psychology majoring in Cognitive Development.

In 1991 he realized a personal ambition and moved to New York where he studied film direction, production and writing for film at New York University. Since then he has written numerous screenplays in several genre and has written, produced and directed many shorts and three feature films, Virgin Cowboys, Magdalen and Jack Gambel: The Enigma.

He later studied creative writing at Oxford University and is presently completing a doctorate of divinity in Metaphysical Science. He is a member of the American Society of Criminology. He has written five books on true crime: Serial Sex Killers, Real American Psychos; Sexual Psychopaths, British Serial Killers; Murder for Profit; and Forensic Science, Crime Scene Analysis. The books were motivated by dual diplomas he had taken in the Psychology of Criminal Profiling and the second in Forensic Science specializing in Crime Scene Analysis.

He lives with his family in London, England.